PLANET CAKE

LOVE AND FRIENDSHIP

PLANET CAKE

LOVE AND FRIENDSHIP

Celebration Cakes
for Special Occasions

PARIS CUTLER

PHOTOGRAPHY BY CHRIS CHEN

MURDOCH BOOKS

CONTENTS

PLANET CAKE LOVE AND FRIENDSHIP

I truly believe there can be no better gift to give someone than a cake. In a world where everything is instant, to make something meaningful with time, care and love means more to the recipient than ever before.

This is my fifth book and it has definitely been the most enjoyable to write, as I have finally had the opportunity to cover my favourite topics: love and friendship. *Planet Cake: Love and friendship* is a sequel to my first book, *Planet Cake: A beginner's guide to decorating incredible cakes*. So many readers wanted me to write a book that included wedding cakes—finally, here it is!

Writing this book was a wonderful challenge. It is always my number one aim to encourage beginners to decorate cakes and to do this we need to eliminate the mystery; every cake can be broken down into a step-by-step process. I have chosen cakes that have been tried and tested in our school and most are classic designs; however, each of the cakes I have chosen uses a different technique. I hope that by learning the fundamentals of these techniques you will be encouraged to design your own cakes. That is my wish for you because the joy of decorating lies in exploring your creative side rather than having to follow a step-by-step instruction book all the time. After a while, you should find you only need to refer back to this book for a technique or two.

Many of our students and all of our interns have gone on to become great decorators in their own right and, without naming people directly, some of them are now among the most well-known cake decorators in the industry. Therefore I feel very confident in saying that you can achieve great results using the instructions in this book. Don't worry about a crack here or there, it is all part of the learning process. Believe me, everyone starts somewhere: even the greatest decorators did not start off creating perfect cakes.

I regard making cakes for people—especially wedding cakes—to be a great honour, and I take the responsibility very seriously. That said, I know for a fact that it's much more special for a couple (not to mention hundreds of dollars cheaper for them) when their wedding cake is made by someone close to them. Before the cake boom and all the TV shows, most celebration cakes were made by friends and family members. I don't want to do myself out of a job, but I think these homemade cakes are the best of all. I can certainly remember all of the cakes made for me by those I love and care about.

However, I must caution you that once people see your gorgeous creations you may find yourself setting up your own cake business. I have seen this happen many times. Just think about it: how many newly engaged couples are at a wedding? Loads, so make sure that you are prepared for an onslaught of requests!

I wish you great success with all of your cakes, whether the designs are taken from this book or not. I would feel honoured if this book were the start of your lifelong love affair with cake decorating.

HOW TO USE THIS BOOK

1 Choose a cake design

2 If you want to mix 'n' match designs, make your choices now

3 Make figurines or flowers (if required)

4 Prepare all the necessary tools, ingredients and equipment

5 Bake the cakes; use a reliable recipe converter app such as The CakeOmeter to get the size you need

6 Make and apply ganache; leave to set overnight

7 Cover the cakes and boards with ready-to-roll fondant icing; leave to set overnight

8 Assemble the tiers

9 Decorate the cake

At first you may be a little daunted by the cake designs in this book; however, I have chosen cakes that I know you can achieve because we have taught all of the techniques in our decorating school. The students always marvel that, once the techniques are broken down step by step, cake decorating is not mysterious or difficult at all and their results are fantastic. I have selected designs that are popular with our customers; therefore you will be creating something that is not only beautiful but modern and fashionable. The cake trend at the moment is for clean-looking cakes.

As you browse through this book you will notice that I have limited the cake shapes to round, square and cupcakes: this allows you the opportunity to start with a single-tier cake and master setting up and covering and to gain some practice before you tackle a tiered or shaped cake. The techniques are used again and again throughout the book to allow you to become familiar with them. I will not be asking you to apply intricate lace piping or to make hundreds of sugar flowers: let's leave that for another day!

The cake-decorating techniques I have included are sugar flowers, simple figurines, cut-outs (cutting out shapes in icing using a template), quilting, easy piped dots and salutations, bows, stencilling, glitter, ruffles, hand-painting, applying diamantés and a few simple three-dimensional decorations. If you find any of these techniques too intimidating, just skip them. For example, instead of decorating a cake elaborately, you could place a simple ribbon and bow at the base of each tier, adorn the top with a beautiful sugar flower (or a fresh one) and it is just stunning.

The cake designs in this book are interchangeable: for example, the engagement cakes might make beautiful anniversary cakes; or you could change one of the three-tier cakes to a two-tier cake. Just follow the advice in the techniques section and use our guides to adjust quantities of both icing and cake. The most important thing is that you achieve great results: so don't bite off more than you can chew, but simplify the design to suit your skill base and level of confidence.

MATERIALS & EQUIPMENT

GANACHING TOOLS

1 Plastic jug

2 Cleaning cloth

3 Palette knives (various sizes)

4 Long serrated bread knife

5 Pastry brush

6 Cake boards (various sizes)

7 Turntable

8 Nonslip rubber mat

9 Baking paper

10 DIY board

11 Pencils (2B)

12 Flexiscraper

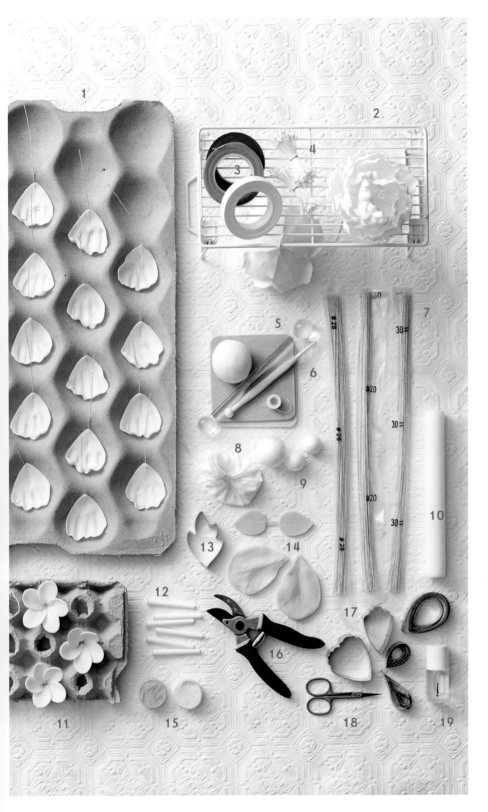

FLOWERMAKING TOOLS

1 Petal drying rack (apple tray)

2 Wire drying rack

3 Florists' stem tape (various colours)

4 Stamens

5 Ball tool and ball tool pad (also known as a petal pad)

6 Frilling tool

7 Florists' wire (various gauges)

8 Cornflour (cornstarch) puffer

9 Polystyrene balls (various sizes)

10 Small rolling pin

11 Flower drying rack (egg carton)

12 Flower picks (posy picks)

13 Peony leaf cutter

14 Petal and leaf veiners

15 Flower dust (pink and yellow)

16 Secateurs

17 Peony, rose and frangipani petal cutters and rose leaf cutters (various sizes)

18 Small scissors

19 Sugar glue

ICING &
DECORATING TOOLS

1　Paintbrushes (various sizes) and paint palette

2　Large rolling pin

3　Diamantés (rope and single)

4　Paring knife

5　Palette knives (various sizes)

6　Baking paper

7　Small silicone rolling pin

8　Marzipan knife

9　Cornflour puffer

10　Toothpicks

11　Butchers' skewers

12　Modelling tools

13　Pastry brush

14　Piping (icing) bags and nozzles

15　Plunger cutters (blossoms, butterflies, leaves, etc.)

16　Cutters (alphabets, numbers, hearts, stars, circles, squares, etc.)

17　Acetate film

18　Florists' wire

19　Stencil

20　Flexiscraper

21　Vinyl sheet

22　Set square

23　Winged acrylic smoothers

24　Pizza cutter

25　Stitching tool, frilling tool

26　Small icing smoother

27　Tape measure

28　Scissors

29　Craft knife

30　Wire-cutter pliers

31　Metal scraper

32　Acrylic ruler and spacers

EDIBLE MATERIALS & DECORATIONS

1 Cake stand

2 Food colouring paste and coloured icing balls (various colours)

3 Coloured sprinkles

4 Cornflour (cornstarch)

5 Gold edible paint

6 Food colouring liquid

7 Ready-to-roll fondant icing in white, red and black

8 Royal icing

9 Cake decorator's alcohol

10 Edible glitter

11 Pastry brush with piping gel

12 Lustre dust

13 Tylose powder

14 Large and small cachous

GLOSSARY

Many items listed here are available from specialist cake-decorating suppliers. Some of the everyday items can be bought at cookware shops or the supermarket.

Acetate film: Often described as plastic film or sheeting. This general-purpose plastic is an industry standard in graphic arts, packaging, printing and for overlays.

Acrylic smoother: This tool has a flat surface and a handle on the back and is used for smoothing air bubbles out of fondant icing and shaping the icing onto the cake.

Acrylic spacers and cardboard templates: Used to help set out decorations evenly, these are available from cake-decorating suppliers, or you can draw up your own.

Baking paper: This nonstick paper is helpful for everything from lining cake tins for baking to making stencils and templates, as it is translucent and easy to trace through.

Ball tool: This plastic handle with a ball at each end is used to make round indentations and smooth curves in soft icing and modelling paste or to shape flower petals.

Ball tool pad (also known as a petal pad): This is a sturdy foam pad for use with the ball tool, and is available from cake-decorating suppliers.

Bread knife: A bread knife is used for slicing cakes into layers. Ideally the knife blade should be 30 cm (12 inches) or longer and serrated.

Butchers' skewers or cake dowels: These are long thin cylindrical plastic or wooden pillars with a point at one end. They are pushed into cakes to support tiers. They are also useful for moulding and modelling. If they are to be inserted into the cake we recommend covering wooden dowels with food-safe tape.

Cachous: Also known as dragees, these are round, edible sugar balls coated with silver, gold or other colours.

Cake boards (various sizes): These boards are usually made from masonite covered with silver or gold foil and are available from cake-decorating suppliers. Set-up boards are the same size as the cake (for example 23 cm (9 inch) round cake goes on a 23 cm (9 inch) round board and they operate as a guide for ganaching and a way to easily handle the cake and not stain the display board. The cake display board is a larger board the cake is placed on as part of its display. It is usually 10–15 cm (4–6 inches) larger than the cake and at Planet Cake we usually cover it with fondant to match the cake.

Cake decorator's alcohol: Also known as rose spirit because it has five per cent rose essence added, it is used for diluting pigments and metallic powders for painting and can also be useful for removing icing stains. Vodka can be a substitute.

Cake stand: A flat platter on a pedestal, often ceramic or glass. Can be used instead of, or as well as, a display board.

Cleaning cloth: An ordinary kitchen cloth comes in handy for tidying up as well as for removing marks and stains on fondant icing.

Cornflour (cornstarch): Used for dusting the work surface when rolling out icing, to make it nonstick. Cornflour must be used sparingly as it can dry out the icing, but it is finer than icing (confectioners') sugar.

Cornflour (cornstarch) puffer: Take a small square of muslin (cheesecloth) and place cornflour in the centre, then draw up the corners and secure the fabric with a rubber band.

Couverture chocolate: Natural, sweet chocolate containing no added fats other than natural cocoa butter. It is used for flavouring ganache, dipping, moulding, coating and similar.

Craft knife: A knife with a retractable, replaceable blade, sometimes known as a Stanley knife or box cutter.

Cutters (alphabets, numbers, hearts, stars, circles, etc.): Available in different sizes and shapes, cutters often come in sets made of plastic or stainless steel. Available from cake-decorating suppliers.

Diamantés: Small plastic or glass faceted pieces that sparkle. They can be bought as indiviual pieces or in ropes.

DIY board: Template cardboard is useful for cutting cakes and icing into a shape.

Edible glitter: Non-toxic glitter is available in a range of colours and is usually adhered with water or piping gel.

Edible metallic dust: Metallic powder is available in petal, pearl, sparkle and lustre finishes. Some decorators mix the powder with cake decorator's alcohol and apply directly. The lustre and pearl powders create a luminous effect on sugar flowers.

Electronic scales: Useful for precise measurements of small amounts of icing, ingredients and decorations.

Flexiscraper: This tool is a Planet Cake invention. We use either unused X-ray film, which can be hard to find, or a thin plastic such as acetate, film or the type used for bendy display folders (the ones with the plastic sleeves inside). Cut your plastic into a rectangle a little larger than the palm of your hand, round the corners using scissors and then sterilise before use.

Florists' stem tape (white, green or brown): The tape can be twisted on its own to create flexible stems, but it can also be used to cover wires or dowels before inserting them into a cake.

Florists' wire: Fine wire used by florists to support flower stems. Can be used to secure petals to sugar flowers and support icing decorations. It is available at cake-decorating suppliers.

Flower drying rack: A plastic-coated wire rack is useful for holding decorations and sugar flowers while they dry out. We also use apple trays and egg cartons (see Petal drying rack).

Flower dust: Coloured edible dust used to add a natural blush to sugar flowers.

Flower petal and leaf cutters and veiners: Common shapes include rose, peony, frangipani and orchids. The veiners are small moulds or presses that add natural-looking texture to precut shapes. Sets available from cake-decorating suppliers.

Food colouring paste or liquid: Paste or gel food colouring is the most concentrated of food colours. Mix this paste directly into fondant icing to colour it or mix it with alcohol to paint on icing. Liquid food colouring is similar but less intense.

Frilling tool: This tool is part of a set called 'modelling tools'. It is used for making sugar flowers and icing figurines and has many applications.

Ganache (dark or white chocolate): This is a mixture of chocolate and cream. It can be made with dark, milk or white chocolate and is used as filling and icing for cakes.

Glaze: A product or mixture that gives a shiny appearance to cakes or decorations.

Glycerine: A colourless, odourless, syrupy liquid made from fats and oils, used to retain moisture and add sweetness to foods. Stir into icing to restore consistency or use to soften fondant or royal icing. It can also be used to soften dried food colourings.

Long-nose pliers: Make sure they have a wire-cutter built in. They are available from any good hardware store.

Lustre dust: See Edible metallic dust.

Marzipan: This almond paste is made from ground blanched almonds mixed with icing (confectioners') sugar. It is used in a very thin layer on fruit cakes before icing.

Marzipan knife: A flexible plastic knife that minimises 'dragging' when cutting icing.

Masking tape: Good quality tape from the hardware store is best as it is strong and will not leave residue when removed.

Metal scraper: Used for smoothing ganache or icing.

Modelling tools: A set of tools with different shaped ends used for shaping fondant for decorations. See also Ball tool and Frilling tool.

Nonslip mats: These mats are perfect for placing under a turntable or cake board to prevent slipping. A mat is also useful when placing a cake in a box for transport.

Paintbrushes (various sizes): Fine paintbrushes can be used for painting, brushing crumbs or icing (confectioners') sugar out of tricky corners, applying water or piping gel as adhesive, as well as applying powdered or liquid colours. Broad brushes are useful for cleaning debris off the cake board.

Palette knives (various sizes): A palette knife is a flat bladed metal knife with a rounded tip used to smooth ganache on cakes and cupcakes. It can also be handy when transferring the cake to the display board. A crank-handled palette knife is a knife with a stepped bend in the blade.

Paring knife: A small kitchen knife with a straight blade, useful for cutting decorations and trimming fondant icing.

Pasta machine: This stainless steel machine is useful for rolling out icing as it provides a consistent thickness and perfect finish.

Pastry brush: A flat brush with coarse bristles, used for applying lustre or piping gel.

Pencil: A 2B pencil is used for tracing designs and transferring images onto icing.

Petal and leaf cutter sets: See Flower petal and leaf cutters and veiners.

Petal drying rack: We use apple trays from the fruit store.

Piping (icing) bags: Made of fabric, or disposable plastic, you can also make your own using baking paper. Start with a square piece, fold into a triangle and roll up the folded side to form a cone shape with no hole. Snip a hole in the tip with scissors and push the piping tip into the bag before filling the bag with royal icing or piping gel.

Piping (icing) tips (various sizes): These are attached to the piping bag to give form to icing decorations. The size and shape of the opening on a piping tip determines the type of decoration the tip will produce. They are sometimes called decorating tubes or tips. A coupler sits between the piping bag and piping tip. You can screw the piping tip onto the coupler, and easily change between different sizes and shapes without changing the piping bag.

Piping gel: This clear, sticky gel becomes fluid when warmed. Used as a glue to adhere decorations or ribbons, it can also be coloured for piping designs on dry sugar paste or royal icing. It maintains a shiny wet look when set and is also known as piping jelly.

Pizza cutter: Used to trim rolled fondant icing neatly.

Plastic jug: Keep a small jug of water handy for cleaning up and also for adhering fondant icing and decorations.

Pliers/wire cutters: See Long-nose pliers.

Plunger cutters (blossoms, butterflies, flowers, leaves, etc.): These are available from cake-decorating suppliers.

Posy picks: Small plastic vessels used to insert fresh flowers without contaminating the cake and icing.

Ready-to-roll fondant icing: Also called RTR, plastic icing, sugar paste and fondant, this is a dough-like icing that is rolled out, draped over the cake and then smoothed down. It is used to cover cakes and cupcakes. Fondant gives the cake a beautiful, porcelain-like surface that can be painted, piped, quilted, cut out or stamped. Fondant comes in white or ivory and can be coloured using food colouring paste. It is also used to model figurines and three-dimensional shapes, such as ribbons, bows and cut-outs. Good quality fondant is costly but worth buying.

Red or black icing: You can colour your own red or black icing, but we advise buying these colours ready-made from a cake-decorating supplier as the colours are more consistent and the icing is easier to use.

Rolling pins: Rolling pins are usually made from wood but can also be made from marble or silicone. Choose a rolling pin you are comfortable with. A rolling pin approximately 55 cm (22 inches) long is ideal. A small rolling pin is useful for rolling out tiny quantities of icing for decorations. You can buy small rolling pins from cake-decorating suppliers, but the most prized ones at Planet Cake are those found in children's baking sets! A variety of rolling pins are available: without handles, with integral handles, or—Planet Cake's favourite—with handles that are attached to a central rod in the barrel of the roller.

Royal icing: A mixture of egg white and icing sugar. It can be spread over cakes and boards and sets very hard. It is also used for piping. You can buy instant royal icing mixes to which you just add water, or you can make your own using the recipe on page 42.

Ruler: A clear acrylic ruler is the most useful for measuring, spacing decorations and quilting lines.

Scissors (various sizes): Used for cutting flowers, ribbons and other decorations as well as making templates.

Scraper (various sizes): Best made of stainless steel, a side scraper is a flat piece of metal or plastic with a straight edge used for scraping any excess ganache off the side of a cake when you are preparing and filling it. Metal scrapers can be sourced from cake-decorating suppliers and the internet. If you don't have a scraper you can use a metal ruler. Plastic scrapers are also fine to use.

Secateurs: Used for cutting fresh flower stems and butchers' skewers.

Set square: Translucent acrylic triangle-shaped measurers are useful for setting up regular angles for decorating, such as when quilting fondant icing.

Smoothers: Also called 'paddles', these rectangular (sometimes rounded on one end, sometimes with turned-up 'wings' on each end) flat plastic smoothers with handles are used for pressing the air bubbles out of fondant icing and rubbing it to a smooth shiny finish. When covering cakes you always need at least two.

Sprinkles: Tiny multicoloured sugar balls are adhered with piping gel or water to icing for a fun effect.

Stamens: The centre parts of sugar flowers are available from cake-decorating suppliers.

Stencils: For applying royal icing or painting on covered cakes, you can make your own designs using stencil plastic or purchase them from cake-decorating suppliers.

Stitching tool: More properly known as a 'tracing wheel', this is an instrument with serrated teeth on a wheel attached to a handle. Used in sewing to transfer markings from paper patterns onto fabric, this tool also makes a perfect stitching effect in fondant icing. Tracing wheels are available from craft stores and haberdashers.

Styrofoam blocks and shapes (balls, eggs, etc.): Available from cake-decorating suppliers, and craft and hobby stores.

Sugar glue: Also called flower glue or edible glue, it is used to adhere dry pieces of fondant icing, such as figurines, to a dried cake. If one or both of the fondant pieces are still soft, they can be stuck with just water, so sugar glue is often not necessary.

Syrup: Sugar syrup or soaking syrup is a mixture made from equal amounts of boiled water and jam (see recipe page 42). The syrup is brushed over the cut surfaces of cakes to prevent them drying out before icing. Syrup can also be flavoured with alcohol such as Cointreau (orange-flavoured liqueur) if you want a stronger taste.

Tape measure: For measuring the circumference of cakes when applying ribbons or calculating the spacing of decorations.

Toothpicks: Used to support figurines and also for marking fine lines on icing.

Turntable: A turntable is a useful tool for when you are coating cakes with royal icing or rolled icing as it allows you to approach the cake from all sides. You can buy a turntable from a cake-decorating supplier but at Planet Cake we use the type that you would put under a television set.

Tylose powder: This setting agent can be mixed into rolled fondant, marzipan or royal icing to form a strong modelling paste that dries hard. It is made of carboxymethyl cellulose (CMC). Tylose powder can also be mixed with a small amount of water to make a thick, strong edible glue.

Vinyl sheet: Use this to cover fondant and flower paste shapes after they have been cut, to prevent them drying out. You can substitute plastic bags or plastic wrap.

Wire: Wire of different thicknesses (called gauges) is available from cake-decorating suppliers. It is sometimes covered with paper.

PLANNING & PREPARATION

CAKE SERVING SIZES

One of the most important steps in your planning is to make sure there is enough cake for everyone. Nothing would be more horrific for the decorator than running out of cake, so err on the side of caution. Take into account how much food the guests will be eating: at a cocktail function I have always found guests are ravenous by the time the cake is served, as they have been busy talking and have not eaten properly. If the occasion is a banquet, usually the thought of another morsel is enough to make the guests explode. Some people are concerned that cake will go to waste; however, compared to running out I would prefer some to be left over. Leftovers can be kept in the freezer or shared with those who could not attend the event. You also need to allow extra if your cake might be cut by someone inexperienced if the venue is not used to serving cake.

SERVING PORTIONS

A finger portion or coffee serving is approximately 2.5 x 5 cm (1 x 2 inches) by the height of the cake; a dessert serving may be either 2.5 x 10 cm (1 x 4 inches) or 5 x 5 cm (2 x 2 inches) by the height of the cake.

ROUND CAKE SERVINGS

15 cm (6 inch) diameter = 12 finger portions
18 cm (7 inch) diameter = 18 finger portions
20 cm (8 inch) diameter = 24 finger portions
23 cm (9 inch) diameter = 32 finger portions
25 cm (10 inch) diameter = 38 finger portions
30 cm (12 inch) diameter = 54 finger portions

SQUARE CAKE SERVINGS

15 cm (6 inch) = 18 finger portions
18 cm (7 inch) = 24 finger portions
20 cm (8 inch) = 32 finger portions
23 cm (9 inch) = 40 finger portions
25 cm (10 inch) = 50 finger portions
28 cm (11 inch) = 60 finger portions
30 cm (12 inch) = 72 finger portions

NOTE: A dessert serving is double the size of a finger portion, so halve the numbers in the tables above if you are using the cake as a dessert.

KITCHEN CAKE

A kitchen cake is usually used at an event to make up additional servings or to provide an alternative flavour, such as a chocolate cake for guests who don't like fruit cake, or a gluten-free option. For additional servings, when the kitchen cake has the same flavour and filling as the main cake, it is generally kept in the kitchen for the caterers to cut during the meal.

CAKE PROPORTIONS

In the cake world certain combinations of sizes are deemed attractive. Some suggestions are given on this page. As a general rule, for a modern elegant cake the lower tiers are 5 cm (2 inches) bigger than the tiers above, while for a traditional cake the lower tiers are 7.5 cm (3 inches) bigger.

For three-tier cakes, I never like to have a larger tier on top than a 15 cm (6 inch) cake, as a bigger top tier can make the overall shape look very squat. For a two-tier cake the largest size I would use on top is an 18 cm (7 inch) cake. When calculating cake dimensions, always begin with the size of the top tier and work your way down;

this way the top tier dictates the overall size of the cake and retains elegant proportions. If you only want a two-tier cake but need extra portions, I would recommend making a kitchen cake rather than a larger top tier. If you get the proportions wrong the cake can look rather chunky: we always aim for elegance and height with our cakes.

If you're using a basic 20–23 cm (8–9 inch) cake recipe, such as the ones in this book, you'll need a reliable recipe converter app (our favourite is CakeOmeter) to help you adjust the quantities for smaller or larger cakes. These apps are available from the app store.

TWO-TIER ROUND CAKE

15 cm (6 inch) + 20 cm or 23 cm (8 inch or 9 inch)
15 cm or 18 cm (6 inch or 7 inch) + 25 cm (10 inch)

TWO-TIER SQUARE CAKE

15 cm (6 inch) + 20 cm or 23 cm (8 inch or 9 inch)
15 cm or 18 cm (6 inch or 7 inch) + 25 cm (10 inch)

THREE-TIER ROUND CAKE

15 cm (6 inch) + 20 cm (8 inch) + 25 cm (10 inch)

15 cm (6 inch) + 23 cm (9 inch) + 30 cm (12 inch)

THREE-TIER SQUARE CAKE

15 cm (6 inch) + 20 cm (8 inch) + 25 cm (10 inch)

15 cm (6 inch) + 23 cm (9 inch) + 30 cm (12 inch)

CAKE CUTTING

The prospect of cutting up your creation may feel daunting, but chances are you will be called upon to do so. There are a few simple rules that will guarantee the whole process will be simple and efficient. Make sure you have made an allowance in your cake portion calculations for cutting errors, so you have room for mistakes.

- Do not attempt to negotiate the cutting in front of guests: remove the cake from the display and take it back to the kitchen or an area that can get messy.

- With very dry hands, remove any figurines, flowers or decorations you would like to keep, wrap them in tissue paper to stop them knocking against each other, and place them in an airtight container.

- If you have a tiered cake, you will normally dismantle the tiers first by gently easing them away from each other.

- Start cutting the biggest tier first.

- Do not try to cut the individual portion sizes directly from the cake: cut larger portions of cake and then cut them further into either fingers or dessert-size portions.

CAKE PRESERVATION

There is a time-honoured tradition of keeping the top tier of a wedding cake for the first christening or anniversary. While I think this is a beautiful sentiment, the reality can be something else. Many couples these days do not want fruit cake, hence it is not possible to keep the cake for this long. If they do have fruit cake and keep the cake, it takes up a lot of freezer space; although I have known couples so committed to the idea they have survived two or three house moves, carting the cake along with them as they go. The third issue is also the reluctance on the part of some people to actually eat a cake that is a year old. But let's push on through: if you are still committed to the idea then it can, of course, be done!

1   To preserve a cake for longer than a few months you need to have a fruit cake treated with marzipan. This request is usually made at the time of ordering. Chocolate cakes can be kept for up to three months in the freezer, with no marzipan required.

2   Make sure your hands and the work surface are completely dry. Remove any sugar flowers or decorations from the cake and place them in an airtight container. Keep the container in a dark cupboard or drawer: the decorations do not require refrigeration; however, they need to be kept away from light to stop them fading and away from moisture which would melt the icing.

3   Wrap the tier you wish to keep in several layers of plastic wrap and make sure every area of cake is securely covered. This ensures no moisture from the freezer damages the icing. If you want to be extra-vigilant, place the wrapped cake in an airtight container, or simply place it in the freezer.

4   When it is time for the cake to see the light of day again, it will take up to 48 hours to defrost. Transfer the frozen cake to the refrigerator first: don't rush the defrosting process or the cake will become soggy. After 8–12 hours in the refrigerator, place the cake on a dry work surface and remove the plastic wrap if it has become a bit soggy. If the cake is wet you can use a fan to dry it.

5   As a final safety precaution, I always lift the cake off the cake board slightly and have a look underneath to make sure everything is truly okay and there is no mould. After getting the all-clear, you can dress the cake using the same sugar flowers as before or new decorations of your choice. Wrap a ribbon around the base to hide the seam and place the cake on a covered cake display board or cake stand, or employ a professional decorator to refinish it.

RECIPES

CAKE RECIPES

The wonderful thing about these cakes is that they actually taste great and retain their moisture and flavour for the days required to decorate them, up to a week.

CHOCOLATE MUD CAKE

Preparation: 15 minutes
Cooking: 1 hour 40 minutes + cooling
Makes: one 23 cm (9 inch) round cake
or one 20 cm (8 inch) square cake

220 g (7¾ oz) butter

220 g (7¾ oz) dark couverture chocolate, chopped

25 g (1 oz / ½ cup) instant coffee granules

125 g (4½ oz) self-raising flour

125 g (4½ oz) plain (all-purpose) flour

50 g (1¾ oz / ⅓ cup) unsweetened cocoa powder

½ teaspoon bicarbonate of soda (baking soda)

480 g (1 lb 1 oz / 1¾ cups) caster (superfine) sugar

4 eggs, lightly beaten

7 teaspoons vegetable oil

100 ml (3½ fl oz) buttermilk

The recipes in this chapter make enough cake batter for a standard 23 cm (9 inch) round cake or a 20 cm (8 inch) square cake. When making smaller and larger cakes, it's crucial to find a good conversion table to help you scale the quantities of ingredients in the cake recipe. There are many reliable conversion apps available for computers and smart devices, but I really like The CakeOmeter.

1 Preheat the oven to 160°C (315°F). Grease the cake tin and line the base and sides with a collar that extends 2 cm (¾ inch) above the top of the tin.

2 Put the butter, chocolate and coffee in a saucepan with 160 ml (5½ fl oz / ⅔ cup) water and stir over low heat until melted, then remove from the heat.

3 Sift the flours, cocoa and bicarbonate of soda into a large bowl. Stir in the sugar and make a well in the centre. Add the combined egg, vegetable oil and buttermilk and the chocolate mixture, stirring with a large spoon until completely combined.

4 Pour the mixture into the tin and bake for 1 hour 40 minutes or until a skewer poked into the centre of the cake comes out clean, though it may be a little sticky. Leave the cake in the tin until cold.

Storage: Keep in an airtight container in the fridge for up to 3 weeks, or freeze for up to 2 months.

WHITE CHOCOLATE MUD CAKE

Preparation: *15 minutes*
Cooking: *1 hour 40 minutes + cooling*
Makes: *one 23 cm (9 inch) round cake*
or one 20 cm (8 inch) square cake

300 g (10½ oz) unsalted butter, chopped
300 g (10½ oz) white couverture chocolate, chopped
300 g (10½ oz/2 cups) plain (all-purpose) flour
150 g (5½ oz/1 cup) self-raising flour
400 g (14 oz/1¾ cups) caster (superfine) sugar
3 eggs, lightly beaten
1½ teaspoons natural vanilla extract

1   Preheat the oven to 180°C (350°F). Grease the cake tin and line the base and sides with a collar of baking paper that extends 2 cm (¾ inch) above the top of the tin.

2   Put the butter and 270 ml (9½ fl oz) water in a saucepan over medium heat and stir until the butter has melted. Turn off the heat, then add the chocolate and stir until it has melted and is well combined.

3   Sift the flours together into a bowl. Add the sugar with a pinch of salt and make a well in the centre.

4   Pour the chocolate mixture, egg and vanilla into the well, then stir with a wooden spoon until well combined.

5   Pour the mixture into the tin and bake for 1 hour 40 minutes or until the cake is golden brown and a skewer comes out clean when poked into the middle of the cake. Cover with foil halfway through if the cake is browning too quickly.

6   Leave to cool completely in the tin on a wire rack.

Storage: Keep in an airtight container in the fridge for up to 1 week, or freeze for up to 1 month.

GLUTEN-FREE BUTTERCAKE

Note: Due to the lack of gluten in this cake, it might sink slightly in the centre during baking. This slight dip can be filled with ganache or buttercream when covering your cake.

Preparation: *15 minutes*
Cooking: *50 minutes + cooling*
Makes: *one 23 cm (9 inch) round cake*
or one 20 cm (8 inch) square cake

250 g (9 oz/1⅔ cups) gluten-free self-raising flour

220 g (7¾ oz/1 cup) caster (superfine) sugar

185 g (6½ oz) unsalted butter, softened

80 ml (2½ fl oz/⅓ cup) milk

4 eggs, at room temperature

1 teaspoon natural vanilla extract

1 Preheat the oven to 180°C (350°F). Grease the cake tin and line the base and sides with baking paper.

2 Sift the flour and 55 g (2 oz/¼ cup) of the sugar into a bowl. Beat the butter in a small bowl using electric beaters for 4–5 minutes until pale and creamy. Gradually beat in the flour and sugar mixture and the milk until just combined. Transfer to a large bowl.

3 Using an electric mixer fitted with the whisk attachment, whisk the eggs, vanilla and remaining sugar in a bowl for about 5–6 minutes until very thick and pale and tripled in volume. Using a spatula or large metal spoon, stir half the egg mixture into the flour mixture. Fold in the remaining egg mixture until just combined.

4 Spoon the mixture into the cake tin and smooth the surface with the back of the spoon. Bake on the centre rack of the oven for 40–50 minutes until a skewer inserted into the centre of the cake comes out clean.

5 Leave the cake in the tin for 10 minutes, before turning out onto a wire rack to cool completely.

Storage: This cake will keep in an airtight container for up to 3 days. It can be frozen, without decoration, for up to 2 months. Wrap tightly in plastic wrap, then place it in a freezer bag and seal. It's a good idea to write the date on the bag.

COCONUT CAKE

Preparation: *15 minutes*
Cooking: *1 hour 40 minutes + cooling*
Makes: *one 23 cm (9 inch) round cake
or one 20 cm (8 inch) square cake*

220 g (7¾ oz) butter, softened
325 g (11½ oz/1¾ cups lightly packed) brown sugar
1 teaspoon natural coconut extract
3 eggs
360 g (12¾ oz) self-raising flour
130 g (4¾ oz/1⅓ cups) desiccated coconut
360 ml (12 fl oz) buttermilk

1   Preheat the oven to 180°C (350°F). Grease the cake tin and line the base and sides with a collar of baking paper that extends 2 cm (¾ inch) above the top of the tin.

2   Beat the butter, sugar and coconut extract until light and fluffy. Add the eggs one at a time, beating well after each addition. Sift the flour and combine with the coconut. Fold in the butter mixture alternating with spoonfuls of buttermilk.

3   Spoon the mixture into the tin and smooth the surface. Bake for 1 hour 10 minutes or until golden brown and a skewer poked into the middle of the cake comes out clean.

4   Leave the cake in the tin for at least 5 minutes before turning out onto a wire rack to cool.

Storage: Keep in an airtight container in the fridge for 1 week, or freeze for up to 2 months.

BANANA CAKE (DAIRY AND EGG FREE)

Note: Due to the density of this cake, it might sink slightly in the centre during baking. This slight dip can be filled with ganache or buttercream when covering your cake.

Preparation: *20 minutes*
Cooking: *1 hour + cooling*
Makes: *one 23 cm (9 inch) round cake
or one 20 cm (8 inch) square cake*

185 g (6½ oz) dairy-free spread
220 g (7¾ oz / 1 cup firmly packed) brown sugar
1 teaspoon natural vanilla extract
360 g (12¾ oz / 1½ cups) mashed banana
 (about 3 large bananas)
45 g (1½ oz / ½ cup) desiccated coconut
300 g (10½ oz / 2 cups) self-raising flour, sifted
1 teaspoon bicarbonate of soda (baking soda)
1 teaspoon mixed spice (all spice)
1 teaspoon ground cinnamon

1 Preheat the oven to 180°C (350°F). Grease the cake tin and line the base and side with baking paper.

2 Cream the dairy-free spread, sugar and vanilla in a small bowl using electric beaters for 3–4 minutes until light and fluffy. Transfer to a large bowl.

3 Using a large metal spoon, fold in the mashed banana and coconut, then the sifted flour, bicarbonate of soda and spices. Stir until just combined and almost smooth.

4 Spoon the mixture into the tin and smooth the surface with the back of the spoon. Bake for 1 hour or until a skewer inserted into the centre of the cake comes out clean.

5 Leave the cake in the tin for 10 minutes, before turning out onto a wire rack to cool completely.

Variation: For a regular banana cake, replace the dairy-free spread with butter, and beat 3 eggs into the creamed butter and sugar mixture. Leave out the coconut and increase the flour by 35 g (1¼ oz / ¼ cup). Bake as directed above.

Storage: This cake will keep in an airtight container for up to 4 days. It can be frozen, without decoration, for up to 2 months. Wrap tightly in plastic wrap, then place in a freezer bag and seal. It's a good idea to write the date on the bag.

VANILLA CUPCAKES

Preparation: *15 minutes + cooling*
Cooking: *25–30 minutes*
Makes: *12*

175 g (6 oz) butter, at room temperature
165 g (5¾ oz/¾ cup) caster (superfine) sugar
½ teaspoon natural vanilla extract
2 eggs, at room temperature
110 g (3¾ oz/¾ cup) self-raising flour, sifted
150 g (5½ oz/1 cup) plain (all-purpose) flour, sifted
160 ml (5½ fl oz/⅔ cup) buttermilk

1   Preheat the oven to 180°C (350°F). Line the holes of a 12-hole 80 ml (2½ fl oz/⅓ cup) muffin tin with paper cases.

2   Beat the butter, sugar and vanilla in a medium bowl using an electric mixer until light and fluffy.

3   Beat the eggs into the butter mixture one at a time. Add half of each of the flours and half the buttermilk, and mix on low speed until just combined. Mix in the remaining flour and buttermilk.

4   Divide the mixture evenly among the paper cases. Gently smooth the tops (this will help the cupcakes rise evenly).

5   Bake for 25–30 minutes until lightly golden and cooked when tested with a skewer. Allow the cupcakes to stand for 5 minutes in the tin before transferring to a wire rack to cool.

CHOCOLATE CUPCAKES

Reduce the plain (all-purpose) flour to 110 g (3¾ oz/¾ cup). Sift 30 g (1 oz/¼ cup) unsweetened cocoa powder and ¼ teaspoon bicarbonate of soda (baking soda) with the flours.

FRUIT CAKE

Preparation: *15 minutes*
Cooking: *2–4.5 hours + cooling*
Makes: *one 15 cm (6 inch) round tier; one 23 cm (9 inch) round tier; one 30 cm (12 inch) round tier*

Small tier

150 g (5½ oz) unsalted butter, plus extra for greasing, softened

90 g (3¼ oz) dark brown sugar

60 g (2¼ oz) caster (superfine) sugar

2 teaspoons natural vanilla extract

5 free-range eggs

165 g (5¾ oz) currants

225 g (8 oz) raisins

340 g (12 oz/2 cups) sultanas (golden raisins)

zest of ½ orange, grated

1 tablespoon treacle

½ teaspoon bicarbonate of soda (baking soda)

185 g (6½ oz/1¼ cups) self-raising flour

½ teaspoon ground cloves

½ teaspoon ground cinnamon

Medium tier

250 g (9 oz) unsalted butter, plus extra for greasing, softened

150 g (5½ oz/¾ cup lightly packed) dark brown sugar

100 g (3½ oz) caster (superfine) sugar

3 teaspoons natural vanilla extract

8 free-range eggs

275 g (9¾ oz) currants

375 g (13 oz) raisins

565 g (1 lb 4 oz) sultanas (golden raisins)

zest of 1 orange, grated

2 tablespoons treacle

¾ teaspoon bicarbonate of soda (baking soda)

310 g (11 oz) self-raising flour

¾ teaspoon ground cloves

¾ teaspoon ground cinnamon

Large tier

375 g (13 oz) unsalted butter, plus extra for greasing, softened

225 g (8 oz) dark brown sugar

150 g (5½ oz/⅔ cup) caster (superfine) sugar

4 teaspoons natural vanilla extract

12 free-range eggs

410 g (14½ oz) currants

550 g (1 lb 4 oz) raisins

850 g (1 lb 14 oz/5 cups) sultanas (golden raisins)

zest of 1½ oranges

3 tablespoons treacle

1 teaspoon bicarbonate of soda (baking soda)

450 g (1 lb/3 cups) self-raising flour

1 teaspoon ground cloves

1 teaspoon ground cinnamon

1 Preheat the oven to 160°C (315°F). Grease and line the base and side of a round cake tin in the appropriate size. I would normally use a couple of layers of brown paper as well as baking paper.

2 Cream the butter, sugar and vanilla together in a bowl until well combined. Gradually beat in the eggs, one at a time, until well combined. Stir in the dried fruit, orange zest and treacle.

3 Sift the bicarbonate of soda, flour and spices together then fold into the mixture until well combined.

4 Spoon the mixture into the cake tin and bake in the oven for about 2 hours (for the small tier), 3 hours (for the medium tier) or 4½ hours (for the large tier). Bake until a skewer inserted into the middle comes out clean.

5 When cooked, remove the cake from the oven and set it aside to cool for 15 minutes. Remove from the tin and place on a wire rack to cool completely.

Storage: Keep in an airtight container in the fridge for up to 1 week, or freeze for up to 1 month.

ICING RECIPES

GANACHE

The ideal chocolate for making ganache is a couverture variety with a cocoa content of 53–63%. In cold weather you might have to add a touch more cream or reduce the chocolate a little bit so that your ganache isn't too hard. If you can't find couverture chocolate, try dark chocolate from the baking section of the supermarket. Do not use thickened (whipping) cream as this contains gelatine.

These recipes make approximately 1.8 kg (4 lb) of ganache, which is enough to cover a standard 20 cm (8 inch) square or 23 cm (9 inch) round cake (with a little left over in case of mishaps).

DARK CHOCOLATE GANACHE

1.2 kg (2 lb 12 oz) dark couverture
   chocolate, finely chopped
600 ml (21 fl oz) pure cream (35% fat)

WHITE CHOCOLATE GANACHE

1.3 kg (3 lb) white couverture chocolate,
   finely chopped
450 ml (16 fl oz) pure cream (35% fat)

Preparation: 15 minutes

STOVETOP METHOD

1   Put the chocolate in a large bowl. Put the cream in a heavy-based saucepan and bring to the boil. Pour the cream over the chocolate and cover with plastic wrap to trap the heat inside.

2   After 2–3 minutes, mix with a whisk until the ganache is smooth and free of lumps. (Do not use an electric mixer, as it will create too many air bubbles.)

3   Cover the surface with plastic wrap and let the ganache cool completely. It is best to leave ganache in the refrigerator overnight to set.

Continued on next page

Ganache continued

MICROWAVE METHOD

1   Put the chocolate and cream in a large microwave-safe bowl. Microwave on medium–high power for 2–3 minutes (the time may vary depending on your microwave).

2   Mix with a whisk until the ganache is smooth and free of lumps. If the mixture still has lumps, return it to the microwave for 1 minute increments until the mixture is completely smooth.

3   Cover the surface with plastic wrap and let it cool completely. It is best to leave ganache to set in the refrigerator overnight.

If the ganache is too hard to spread on the cake it can be brought back to a workable consistency by heating it in the microwave oven. It should have the consistency of peanut butter. Heat as much as you need in the microwave in short bursts of 10–20 seconds; stir after each burst and make sure not to burn or curdle the ganache. Alternatively, put the ganache in a small saucepan over low heat and stir until softened.

The ganache recipe makes enough for one cake, with a bit left over in case anything goes wrong. I like to make a big batch of ganache and decant it into smaller containers to be frozen. If you are planning on using the ganache within a few days, keep it in the refrigerator and allow it to return to room temperature before using. You can keep it in the refrigerator for up to a week, but do check the use-by date on the cream to make sure of the shelf life of the ganache.

READY-TO-ROLL FONDANT

Recipe courtesy of Greg Cleary

15 g (½ oz) powdered gelatine
125 ml (4 fl oz/½ cup) liquid glucose
25 ml (1 fl oz/5 teaspoons) glycerine
1 kg (2 lb 4 oz) icing (confectioners') sugar
2 drops flavour extract (optional)

1 Sprinkle the gelatine over 3 tablespoons of water in a heatproof bowl. Set aside until the gelatine is spongy.

2 Stand the bowl over a saucepan of hot water, ensuring that the base of the bowl does not touch the water, and stir until the gelatine has completely dissolved. Add the glucose and glycerine and stir until melted. Strain through a sieve.

3 Sift the icing sugar into a large bowl, make a well in the centre and pour in the gelatine mixture. Stir until it becomes too difficult to move the spoon. Tip the mixture out onto a clean work surface and add the flavouring, if using. Knead with dry hands into a smooth and pliable dough.

4 Wrap the icing in plastic wrap and store in an airtight container in a cool place (do not refrigerate).

5 Knead again before using, adding more sifted icing sugar if necessary.

ROYAL ICING

1 eggwhite
200–225 g (7–8 oz) icing (confectioners')
   sugar, sifted

1 Put the eggwhite in a clean ceramic, glass or stainless steel bowl that is completely free from any grease.

2 Using an electric mixer fitted with the whisk attachment, whisk on medium speed until frothy. Change to the beater attachment and gradually add the icing sugar until the desired consistency is achieved. The icing is ready when soft peaks form.

3 If mixing by hand, add the icing sugar to the eggwhite 1 teaspoon at a time, beating well. Continue adding icing sugar and beating until the icing reaches soft-peak stage.

4 Store the mixture in an airtight container. Keep in a cool place, but do not refrigerate.

5 It can be used immediately and is best when freshly made.

SYRUP

100 g (3½ oz / ⅓ cup) apricot jam
100 ml (3½ fl oz) boiling water
2 teaspoons Cointreau (orange flavoured liqueur)
   (optional)

1 Mix all of the ingredients together with a whisk until smooth.

2 Store the syrup in an airtight container until ready to use.

FLOWER PASTE

Recipe courtesy of Greg Cleary

300 g (10½ oz) icing (confectioners') sugar

2 teaspoons Tylose powder

½ teaspoon cream of tartar

2 teaspoons gelatine

1 eggwhite

1 tablespoon melted Copha (white
   vegetable shortening)

2 teaspoons liquid glucose

1   Combine the icing sugar, Tylose powder and
    cream of tartar in a bowl and mix well.

2   Put the gelatine in a small bowl with 25 ml
    (5 teaspoons) cold water, stirring until well
    combined. Microwave on medium for 1 minute
    until the gelatine is completely dissolved.
    Add to the icing sugar mixture along with
    the eggwhite.

3   Combine the Copha and glucose, add to the
    mixture and beat in an electric mixer fitted
    with the paddle attachment on high speed
    for 5 minutes.

4   Store in an airtight container in the fridge until
    ready to use.

*I make this in a double batch, but use only 500 g
(1 lb 2 oz) icing (confectioners') sugar. It comes
out quite 'tacky', but I knead it up to the correct
consistency with an extra 100 g (3½ oz) icing
sugar just before using.*

PREPARING CAKES

THREE-DAY RULE

At Planet Cake we follow the three-day rule:

Day one: bake the cake and allow cooling time (or freeze);

Day two: cut and ganache the cake and allow setting time;

Day three: cover the cake with fondant icing and allow setting time.

GANACHING CAKES

CUPCAKES

Ganaching cupcakes extends their life span and ensures that they are moist and delicious. This is especially important if people will be eating cupcakes after the event that you're decorating them for; for example, school fetes and children's parties. Ganache also builds up the cupcake so it is perfectly uniform in spite of any imperfections that may have appeared during baking.

MATERIALS

cupcakes

20 g (¾ oz) ganache, per cupcake

hot water

EQUIPMENT

ganaching tools (see page 12)

1   If the cupcakes have spilled over their paper cases or are uneven, trim the tops so that they are even: it is very difficult to ice a high-domed cupcake.

2   Have the ganache at a workable consistency (see page 40). Using a small palette knife, place a dollop of ganache in the centre. Start working the ganache towards the outside edge of the cake, making sure not to contaminate the paper case with ganache, particularly if you are using dark chocolate.

3   By the time you have ganached the last cupcake, the first cupcakes should be set and ready to hot knife. Dip the palette knife in hot water and smooth the ganache until you have perfect domes.

ROUND CAKES

> It can be helpful to get down to the level of your cake to determine if there are any discrepancies in height.

MATERIALS

round cake
syrup
ganache (see table on page 216
   for quantity)
hot water

EQUIPMENT

ganaching tools

1 Trim the crust from the cake and slice off the top so it is flat. Cut the cake into three slices from the side of the cake.

2 Place the three layers of cake on the work surface and brush each fairly liberally with syrup.

3 Put a dollop of ganache in the middle of a layer of cake. Using the crank-handled palette knife, spread the ganache out towards the edge of the cake. Do the base layer of the cake first. Ensure that the palette knife is only touching the top of the ganache and not the surface of the cake. Each layer of ganache should be around 5 mm (¼ inch) thick at this stage. When you sandwich the three layers back together, put the top layer in the middle, as this will give you a smoother surface to work on for the top.

4 Using a dollop of ganache in the centre of a cake board the same size as the cake, stick the sandwiched cake to the board. Ganache the entire cake, beginning with the side and paying special attention to any holes and gaps.

5 Begin with a thin layer, followed by a thicker rough layer, ensuring that none of the silver board is showing. Use a turntable to spin the cake as you go, ensuring that your hands touch only the turntable and not the cake. Scrape away any excess ganache using a metal scraper.

6 Repeat the process on the top of the cake.

7 Use a knife dipped in hot water and dried (you only want the heat from the water) to get a smooth finish.

SQUARE CAKES

MATERIALS

square cake

syrup

ganache (see table on page 216
  for quantity)

hot water

EQUIPMENT

ganaching tools

1 Trim the crust from the cake and slice off the top so it is flat. Cut the cake into three slices from the side of the cake.

2 Place the three layers of cake on the work surface and brush each fairly liberally with syrup.

3 Put a dollop of ganache in the middle of a layer of cake. Using the crank-handled palette knife, spread the ganache out towards the edges of the cake. Do the base layer of the cake first. Ensure that the palette knife is only touching the top of the ganache and not the surface of the cake. Each layer of ganache should be around 5 mm (¼ inch) thick at this stage. When you sandwich the three layers back together, put the top layer in the middle, as this will give you a smoother surface to work on for the top.

4 Using a dollop of ganache in the centre of a cake board the same size as the cake, stick the sandwiched cake to the board. Ganache the entire cake, beginning with the sides and paying special attention to any holes and gaps.

5 Begin with a thin layer, followed by a thicker rough layer, ensuring that none of the cake board is showing. Scrape away any excess ganache using a metal scraper.

6 Repeat the process on the top of the cake.

7 Use a knife dipped in hot water and dried (you only want the heat from the water) to get a smooth finish.

MARZIPAN

Although none of the cakes in this book use marzipan
I would feel remiss if I did not include instructions for
those wishing to preserve a fruit cake, or for diehard
marzipan fans. A good quality store-bought marzipan
is my preference. The quantity given here will cover
a 20 cm (8 inch) round fruit cake.

MATERIALS

20 cm (8 inch) round cake
800 g (1 lb 12 oz) marzipan
apricot jam, warmed
500 g (1 lb 2 oz) royal icing
   (optional)

EQUIPMENT

pastry brush
rolling pin
paring knife
20 cm (8 inch) cake board
smoothers

1   Turn the cake upside down on the board and trim the cake if it is
    uneven. Roll some marzipan into a sausage and fill in any holes
    in the fruit cake. Brush the cake all over with apricot jam.

2   Roll out a strip of marzipan a bit longer than the cake
    circumference and slightly higher than the side of the
    cake. Cut one long edge of the marzipan straight and roll the
    strip onto a small rolling pin. Unroll the strip around the cake.

3   Trim the marzipan so the join is flush. Cut the top edge of the
    marzipan strip level with the cake top.

4   Roll out a piece of marzipan about 5 cm (2 inches) larger than the
    cake and lay it on a board. Place the cake upside down on top of
    the rolled-out marzipan. Trim away the excess marzipan and turn
    the cake upright again. Smooth the side and the top of the cake.

5   If the cake is a bit uneven at this point, any holes can be filled
    with royal icing. The cake needs to sit for a day to crust over
    before it can be covered with fondant icing.

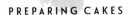

COVERING CAKES

It is very important to learn how to cover your cake professionally, as cakes only taste first-rate if the icing is thin and the cake is moist. Our trainees devote enormous amounts of time to perfecting their covering skills and we place strong emphasis on making sure our cakes are perfectly covered before we decorate them. Please remember that practice makes perfect: by the time you have covered three cakes they will start to look better than most of the cakes you can buy commercially, so don't be put off by a bumpy first attempt.

There are many free videos online and also on the Planet Cake website—planetcake.com.au—if you would like to see a demonstration of covering a cake with fondant. Please bear in mind that buttercream cakes follow a slightly different process than if you are using ganache.

Using a flexiscraper

WHAT IS FONDANT ICING?

Fondant is a creamy white sugar icing, a thick mass used in different forms for the purpose of confectionery and cake decorating. There are different types of fondants, such as rolled fondant, sculpted fondant and poured fondant. For covering cakes we use rolled fondant as it leaves a perfectly smooth, satiny surface and is ready to use: a common product description is 'Ready-to-roll' or RTR. Fondants are sometimes flavoured and there are a variety of different brands. At Planet Cake we buy our rolled fondant icing as the product is good and the recipe is designed for our country's climate. You should be able to buy rolled fondant from most cake-decorating suppliers; however, if you wish you can also make it yourself (see page 41).

To work out the quantity of fondant icing you need, refer to the table on page 216.

IMPORTANT RULES

You will need to follow some very important rules when managing fondant icing.

1   Icing will dry out very quickly, so it is important to work quickly to avoid the icing becoming cracked and difficult to use.

2   When you are not using the icing (even for a minute) put it in a plastic bag or cover it with a vinyl sheet to avoid it drying out.

3   If you have hot hands this will tend to make the icing sticky and then you will be tempted to overuse cornflour (cornstarch) which will dry the icing. Cool your hands under cold water and keep the cornflour to a light sprinkling.

4   Weather will affect the fondant: humidity will make it sticky and very cold weather will make it as hard as rock. We often wait a day if we have bad fondant weather.

5   Never refrigerate a cake after it has been covered, as the fondant will sweat in the fridge. Once the cake is covered it is perfectly fine to store in a cool place at about 20°C (68°F).

6   Store excess fondant icing in a sealed bag or container. Please follow the manufacturer's instructions on how to store: we store ours at room temperature.

7   Safety first: always work fondant icing in small amounts and try to get above the icing when you knead it on the bench. If you are short get a stool so you can use your body weight to help you knead. If you try to knead large amounts of icing you will put pressure on your wrists and make your job very difficult.

8   Never cover a cake straight from the refrigerator: to achieve a professional finish only cover cakes at room temperature.

9   Never use icing that is too dry or over-kneaded, as this will make the corners crack very easily. (See Troubleshooting, page 68.)

10 When making dark colours—such as red, black, brown and purple—make them the day before so the icing has time to relax and rest. (See Techniques, page 72.)

PLANET CAKE'S SECRET WEAPON

The number one question I am asked by students and other decorators is how we achieve such clean edges on our cakes. Is there a secret? I am probably going to surprise you by telling you that there is: we call it a flexiscraper! In an attempt to get an ever more perfect covering result we wanted to find a polishing tool for the icing. After experimenting with all sorts of materials we discovered that by using a thin piece of flexible rounded plastic, similar to acetate or overhead projector film, we could achieve superior results. Using it for buffing and polishing the icing allows us to create razor sharp edges and, because it is flexible, we can smooth the hard-to-navigate icing of shaped and complex cakes. By eliminating all the air bubbles and bumps in the icing the result is a smooth perfect finish.

ROUND CAKES

Round cakes are the easiest to cover. Make sure the cake is ganached and the ganache has set overnight before you attempt to cover your cake. The better the ganache preparation the better your cake will look.

1   Wipe the work surface clean and make sure it is dry. Measure the cake (side and top surface). Place the cake board on a nonslip mat or a moist tea towel (dish towel) so that it does not slip while you are working on it.

2   Brush the cake all over with a little syrup (see page 42). This helps the fondant stick.

3   Knead the fondant icing (add colour if desired: see decorating techniques) to a pliable dough, using a sprinkling of cornflour (cornstarch) if it is sticky. Making sure the icing is smooth, flatten the icing first with the palm of the hand to about 4 cm (1½ inch) thickness before rolling it with a rolling pin (this makes it easier to roll, and in the long run it will save damage to your wrists).

4   Dust a little cornflour on the work surface and roll the icing, starting from the centre. Roll about six times in one direction.

5   Turn the icing, and repeat the process. If the work surface gets sticky use a bit more cornflour but never use cornflour on top.

6   Keep on rolling and turning until the fondant icing is about 3–5 mm (⅛–¼ inch) thick and larger than the total cake measurement.

7   Pick up the icing by rolling it onto a rolling pin (see photo), using a dry pastry brush to remove any excess cornflour (this is particularly important if you use dark coloured icing). Lift the rolling pin with the icing up and unroll it over the cake starting from the base of the cake.

8   Quickly run your hands over the top surface to make sure there are no air bubbles. Secure the edges by running the palms of your hands along the top edge and side of the cake.

9   Press the icing gently against the side. Working around the cake inch by inch, gently pull the icing away from the side of the cake before smoothing it down.

Kneading icing is not like kneading dough: if you keep pummelling, it will stick to the work surface and become unmanageable. Treat your icing like modelling dough: keep folding it in until it is smooth and warm but does not stick to the work surface.

* * * * * * * * * * * * * * * *

Turning the icing will ensure that the sheet will always be a square, which will make covering a round or square cake much easier.

10 Once the whole cake is covered, take a cake smoother and gently press the remaining icing against the side and base of the cake to make a cutting line.

11 Trim the excess icing using a small sharp knife or a pizza cutter.

12 Run a smoother along the side of the cake. I use two smoothers to do this job: the one in the left hand is running back and forth and the one on the right hand is pressed against the cake to make a sharp edge (see photo on page 55). Hold one smoother on the side of the cake and the other one on the top surface, giving the same amount of pressure. Press them together and run them along the side of the cake so as to give a sharp edge.

13 Glide your hand along the cake: if you can feel any air bubbles use a small pin to gently take the air out, then go over it with a smoother or flexiscraper to buff and polish the icing.

Do not trim the icing too close to the base of your cake as the icing shrinks up and you could be left with a gap. If this does happen, adjust your design and place a roll of icing or a ribbon around the base of the cake (see cake-decorating techniques, page 77).

CUPCAKES

1 Roll out the icing to 3 mm (⅛ inch) thick using a pasta machine or a rolling pin. Cut out circles with a round cutter in the closest size to the diameter of the cupcakes. Keep the icing discs covered with a vinyl sheet or in a resealable plastic bag to prevent them drying out.

2 Brush each ganached cupcake with syrup and adhere an icing disc over the top. Push the icing into place until it sits perfectly on the surface of the cupcake, then use a flexiscraper to smooth the icing.

SQUARE CAKES

Use the same guidelines when covering a square cake as for the round cake.

1. The most important technique is to secure the corners immediately, as soon as the icing is on the cake (see photo).

2. Use both hands and work on the corners first: push the icing right down the corners.

3. Now manipulate the icing on the straight side to achieve a neat finish.

4. Once the icing is trimmed all around the base, use the acrylic smoothers as for the round cake. For a sharp edge use two flexiscrapers and work them against each other (see photo).

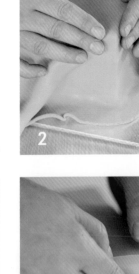

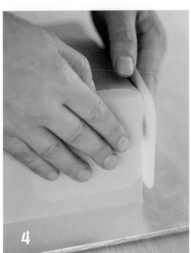

HOW TO COVER A CAKE BOARD

Let me make it clear that you do not need to cover the board in icing: in fact, many decorators don't. At Planet Cake we choose to cover our boards because we believe it looks much cleaner and we don't particularly like the look of silver or gold boards as we feel they undermine the cake.

1   Roll the icing to about 3 mm (⅛ inch) thick and to at least the same size as the board.

2   Lay the icing on the board (if it is too small, keep on rolling it on the board till it covers the whole surface). Dip a pastry brush in some water, lift the icing half way up and brush the board. Lay the icing down and do the same to the other side. Use the flexiscraper or the acrylic smoother to go over the surface and create a neat finish. Trim most of the excess icing with scissors.

3   Place the iced board on a turntable or half way over the table edge. Hold an acrylic smoother at a 45-degree angle and slide it along the edge to cut the icing: this will give you a nice bevelled edge (see photos 3a and 3b).

4   Let the board dry before you stack the cake on it, adhering the cake with a dab of ganache. There is no need to remove the cake board you were using when applying the ganache.

For a perfect finish, add a narrow ribbon around the edge of the board by placing the board on a turntable and applying glue-stick adhesive or double-sided adhesive tape around the edge to hold the ribbon. Make sure the join is at the back of the board. You can use plain or patterned ribbon for additional decoration.

TRANSFERRING THE CAKE TO THE COVERED BOARD

1   Using a plain cake board the same size as your cake, place it on the iced board. Use a ruler to make sure the board is placed with even space around it. Scribe along the edge of the board with a frilling tool.

2   Lift the plain cake board off to reveal a clear marking showing where to place the cake.

3   Using a paring knife, lever the cake from the board and place it on the marked area on the covered board.

ASSEMBLING & STACKING TIERED CAKES

EQUIPMENT

cake board (same size as
   top tier)
ruler
frilling tool
butchers' skewers
pencil
secateurs
royal icing (see page 42)
large and small crank-handled
   palette knives

1   Place the cake on a temporary cake board. Place a plain cake board the same size as the top tier in the centre of the bottom tier and use a ruler to ensure that it is centred. Trace around the cake board to scribe an outline in the icing of the bottom tier and remove the cake board.

2   Insert four butchers' skewers into the bottom tier, equally spaced out and just inside the scribed outline.

3   Use a pencil to mark the height of the cake on the skewers.

4   Use secateurs to snip off the length of the butchers' skewers just below the marked height.

5   Replace the skewers in the cake, pushing them all the way in. Prepare a small amount of royal icing to help stick the top tier onto the bottom tier.

6   Spread the royal icing inside the scribed circle using a small crank-handled palette knife.

7   Use the large crank-handled palette knife to lift and help position the top tier on the bottom tier, aligning the edges with the scribed outline.

TROUBLESHOOTING & TECHNIQUES

TROUBLESHOOTING

BAKING

Baking is a science. Everything must be just right to bake the perfect cake: the measurements, the temperature, the procedure. Getting just one thing wrong can often lead to mishaps, such as a burnt cake, a collapsed cake or one that doesn't want to come out of the tin. These troubleshooting tips will ensure you bake the perfect cake every time.

OVENS

A fan-forced (convection) oven is an oven that has fans to circulate air around food. If you have a fan-forced oven, reduce the temperature in the recipe by 20°C (35°F). Fans help distribute heat evenly around the food, removing the blanket of cool air that surrounds food in an oven, allowing food to cook more evenly in less time and at a lower temperature than in a conventional oven. Conventional ovens, which do not have fans, rely primarily on radiation from the oven walls, to transfer heat.

MEASURING INGREDIENTS

Measure all ingredients first and ensure ingredients are at room temperature. Use scales for accuracy rather than a measuring jug or cups.

LINING THE CAKE TIN

You should always line your cake tin because it makes all the difference whether a cake will slide out easily or stick right in. For round tins, trace the base onto baking paper and cut out the circle, then cut a strip to fit around the side of the tin. For square tins, add the height of the sides to the base measurement and cut a square this size, snipping the corners diagonally. Grease the tin and press the lining into the base and sides.

OPENING THE OVEN DOOR

Resist the urge to open the oven door during baking, as the heat will fluctuate and may cause the cake to sink. If you can, turn the oven light on and view the cake through the oven window.

TESTING FOR A PERFECTLY BAKED CAKE

TOUCH METHOD: Gently press the centre of the cake; if it springs back the cake is cooked.

SKEWER METHOD: Insert a clean wooden skewer into the centre of the cake. If the skewer comes out clean, the cake is cooked. If there is cake batter stuck to the skewer, return the cake to the oven until baked thoroughly.

STORING CAKES

If using the cake straight away, wait until it has cooled before wrapping it. If using the cake the next day, allow it to cool then wrap it in nonstick baking paper, then plastic wrap; this seals in freshness. If freezing the cake, let it cool then wrap in nonstick baking paper, then plastic wrap, then a layer of foil as a protective layer, or place it in an airtight container to reduce freezer burn.

WHY DO CAKES SINK?

- Cakes usually sink when the batter is not completely cooked. Ovens are all different so you need to find the optimum baking time for your oven.

- Overbeating the batter and incorporating too much air can cause a collapse in the mixture.

- If the temperature of the oven is too high, it causes the cake to rise too rapidly. Invest in an oven thermometer to check your oven temperature.

- Opening the oven door to check on the cakes before the batter is set can cause the cake to sink, as can closing the oven door too sharply in the early stages of baking.

- Placing baked cakes to cool in a draughty place can also cause sinking.

WHY IS MY CAKE BURNT?

- Oven temperature is too high: bake at a slightly lower temperature for a bit longer.

- Cover the cake batter with foil before baking or if it is starting to colour too much.

- Wrap the sides of the cake tin with newspaper or brown paper to insulate the tin: this works very well for fruit cakes, as they require a longer baking time.

- Your oven may have a hot spot: it is best to turn your cake around during baking or move it to a different shelf if this is the case.

WHY IS MY CAKE DOMED?

- Overmixing the cake batter, causing the eggs to rise rapidly like a soufflé.

- Hot spot in the oven.

- Cake batter not poured evenly into the tin.

Cut the dome off the top of the cake and build up the edges of the cake with icing to ensure an even level. Use the offcuts for something else.

TROUBLESHOOTING GANACHE

Ganache is made by heating cream and pouring it over chopped dark chocolate. The mixture is stirred or blended until smooth and the chocolate is melted. The flavour of ganache can be enhanced with liqueurs or extracts. Depending on the kind of chocolate used, the amount of cream should be adjusted to give the desired consistency.

The skilful ganaching and cutting of cakes is the real secret behind the quality of Planet Cake's success. No amount of fancy decoration can disguise a badly set up or lumpy cake. Although a little tricky at first, with practice you will master the skills; whether you want to make amazing cakes for friends and family or start up a commercial venture, you will be setting up your cakes in the knowledge that you are striving for the best possible results.

I know that ganache works: clients love the flavour, it keeps the cakes moist, it looks fantastic and, once it has been applied, the cake does not require refrigeration, making it convenient and commercial. Ganache allows us to set up cakes up to four days ahead of their eating date and becomes a delicious and effective adhesive with complex cakes. I usually explain the benefits of ganache by using the analogy of wall putty. In order for Planet Cake to achieve our enviable sharp edges and to keep the fondant icing thin, the cake needs to be perfect before it is covered.

Ganache acts like putty and fills in all of the holes and divots in your cake. Once the ganache has set hard and is perfectly smooth, it presents a firm and perfect surface for covering with thinly rolled fondant icing, thus achieving a professional and delicious result.

GANACHE VS BUTTERCREAM

Alternative: If you are currently using buttercream icing under fondant and want to continue, please do; however, it's unlikely that you will get clean edges, as buttercream does not set like ganache and it is this quality that is the key advantage.

WHAT IS THE DIFFERENCE BETWEEN WHITE AND DARK GANACHE?

We suggest pairing dark chocolate ganache with chocolate cakes and heavier cake flavours, while white chocolate ganache is sweeter and is best paired with lighter textured and flavoured cakes such as white chocolate cakes or carrot cakes; however, you might want to experiment with your own combinations.

White chocolate ganache is less stable than dark chocolate ganache, so in hot weather and for complex cakes we recommend sticking with dark chocolate ganache to ensure your cake will set.

WHAT TYPE OF CHOCOLATE SHOULD I USE?

We use couverture chocolate with 53–63% cocoa content. Please make sure that you don't use chocolate with a very high cocoa content; if the cocoa content is too high it burns easily and curdles very quickly; the taste will be very bitter; and it will set very hard as it only has a little cocoa butter in it. It is best to have the chocolate chopped finely so that it melts evenly.

WHAT TYPE OF CREAM DO YOU USE TO MAKE GANACHE?

We normally use pure cream (35% fat: thin or pouring cream) for making ganache; you can use thickened (whipping) cream as a last resort; however, this contains gelatine and will make the job a little more difficult. As a general rule, use a cream with a low fat content, which does not thicken when beaten.

CAN YOU MAKE GANACHE IN A MICROWAVE OVEN?

Yes, absolutely. See microwave method instructions on page 40.

HOW LONG DOES GANACHE KEEP FOR?

Ganache will normally stay fresh for a week; however, it's always wise to check the use-by dates of the cream you are using and make sure it has at least a week's shelf life.

HOW DO YOU STORE GANACHE?

We recommend making a big batch of ganache and then decanting it into smaller containers and freezing the leftovers. If you are planning to use the ganache within a few days of making it, keep it in the refrigerator for guaranteed safety and bring it to room temperature before using.

HOW DO YOU REHEAT GANACHE?

Keep the ganache in smaller containers and heat just as much as you need in the microwave, making sure not to 'cook' it, which would result in a curdled appearance and the ganache would be spoilt.

HOW DO I KNOW IF THE GANACHE IS OFF?

The ganache may appear curdled and will taste sour due to the cream going off. It is best to taste the ganache prior to using if you are unsure.

SETTING GANACHE

It is imperative to let ganache set before you smooth it with a hot knife or cover it with fondant: the ganache should feel firm and fairly solid to the touch. This usually takes at least an hour in cool temperatures. You can speed up the setting time by placing the cake in the refrigerator or freezer for a maximum of 10 minutes for cakes and 5 minutes for cupcakes; however, this is not best practice as it could cause the cake to sweat.

For best results, let the ganache set before hot knifing and then allow it to dry out overnight before covering with rolled fondant icing.

TROUBLESHOOTING FONDANT ICING

STICKY ICING

Due to humidity, icing often becomes soft and sticky.
To solve this, mix sifted icing (confectioners') sugar into the icing a little at a time and knead it through.

ICING TOO DRY

If the icing is dry and cracking, apply a little water to it using a brush, then knead it through. Alternatively, brush the fondant icing with a small amount of glycerine (see Glossary, page 19) and knead it through.

AIR BUBBLES

Feel over the icing surface for air bubbles: lightly prick any bubbles with a pin to let the air escape, then smooth over the icing with a flexiscraper. Always try to eliminate air bubbles under your icing as they will get bigger and lift the icing.

ICING TOO WET

Wet icing is usually the result of too much colour pigment; therefore black, red and brown icing often become 'wet' and difficult to work with. To solve this, knead a little sifted icing (confectioners') sugar into the icing a tiny bit at a time until it becomes less sticky but is still pliable.

CLEANING STAINED ICING

1A. CORNFLOUR STAIN

Apply decorating alcohol to the stain with a soft paintbrush. The alcohol will absorb the cornflour (cornstarch). Pat dry with a soft tissue.

1B. CHOCOLATE STAIN

Use a soft paintbrush to wash the stained area lightly with a very small amount of warm soapy water.

2. DRY WITH A TISSUE

Rinse the brush and wash the soap away with clean water. Lightly dry with a tissue.

3. DUST WITH CORNFLOUR

Lightly dust the area with cornflour (cornstarch) using a soft brush.

MENDING TORN ICING

1. GAP IN ICING

Tearing is usually the result of smoothing and pulling your icing down too vigorously when covering.

2. SMOOTH THE TEAR

While the icing is still soft, use your hands and a flexiscraper to massage the icing up and around the tear so that the gap is closed and almost invisible. If you are still left with a hole, wait until the icing has dried (the next day). Make a small ball of fresh icing in the same colour as your base and massage the fresh icing into the tear like putty. Smooth with a flexiscraper and allow to dry.

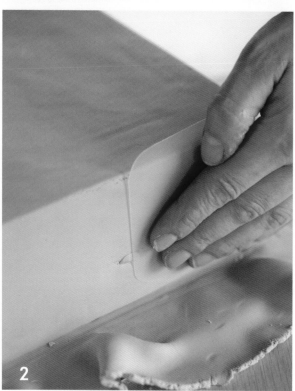

MENDING CRACKED ICING

Cracks usually appear on corners or edges when the icing is too dry. While the icing is still soft, use very warm hands to massage the icing inwards around the cracks, closing them and rendering them almost invisible.

COVERING CRACKED ICING

A huge crack is impossible to fix completely, but you can cover it up with some decorations such as flowers so nobody will notice it.

TECHNIQUES

COLOURING FONDANT ICING

Tint a small ball or enough to cover a whole cake. The important thing is to add just a little of the concentrated icing colour at a time, until you arrive at the exact shade you want. Make sure you have enough for the whole cake, as matching the original colour can be an impossible task.

1. GATHER INGREDIENTS

Begin with a kneadable amount of white fondant icing and concentrated icing colouring. There are many different brands and types of icing colouring and it is easy to become confused. We recommend colouring paste to colour rolled fondant icing.

2. ADD COLOUR

Roll the fondant into a ball, kneading until it is soft and pliable. Using a toothpick or palette knife, add dots of colouring paste. You can make more elaborate colours by mixing different icing colours together: a colour wheel can help you choose which colours to mix.

3. KNEAD

Knead the colouring paste into the fondant; be sure to wear gloves to keep your hands stain-free. When the colour appears evenly blended, cut the icing ball in half with a paring knife to check.

4. CONTINUE BLENDING

Continue kneading until the colour is evenly blended and appears as a solid colour all the way through the icing ball.

Intense colours: When making deep colours, such as brown, orange or royal blue, use larger amounts of food colouring paste than normal. It is best to make dark coloured icing a day ahead, as the icing will be exceptionally soft due to the large amount of pigment in it. We recommend buying ready-made red and black fondant icing.

Prevent fading: pinks are especially susceptible to fading out after the cake is finished. Pink and mauve can be reduced to almost white when exposed to sunlight, while purples fade to blue, blues to grey, and black to purple or green. Be careful to protect your cake from light, either by placing it in a cake box immediately or covering it with a cloth.

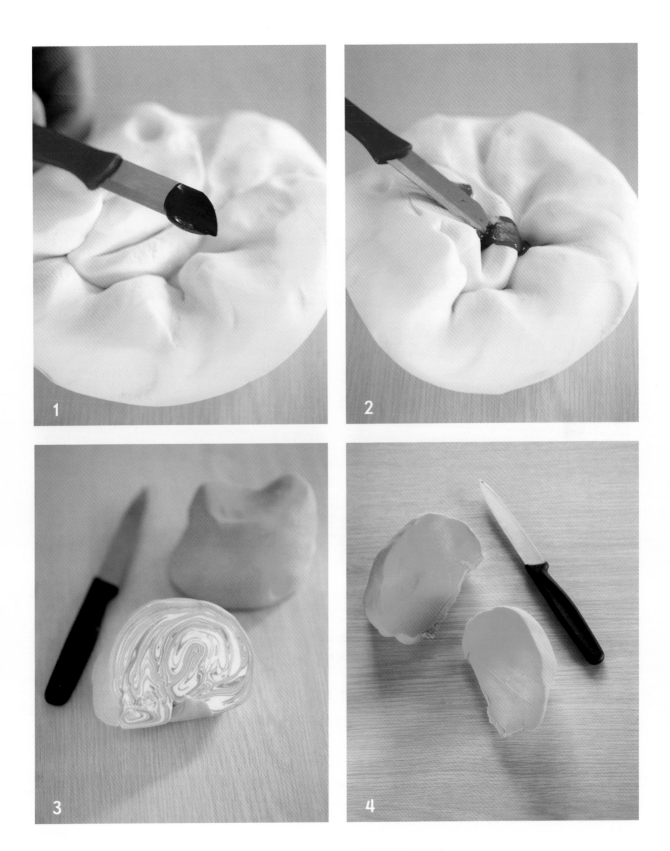

PASTA MACHINE

Each pasta machine is different so you will need to experiment to work out which setting will roll your icing to 3 mm (⅛ inch), which is the desired thickness for most cake decorating purposes.

1. KNEAD AND ROLL

Knead a piece of icing and roll it flat using a small rolling pin. Place the flattened piece in the pasta machine.

2. TURN THE CRANK

Roll the icing through the pasta machine and repeat if necessary until you end up with the desired thickness.

3. CREATE EFFECTS

Your pasta machine should also have settings that will create narrow strips for ribbons, tassels or hair and other great effects. Make sure to keep the pasta machine clean, especially after rolling strong colours.

GLAZING ICING

For glazing, use jam diluted with boiling water (strain to remove any lumps), or olive oil cooking spray. Apply with a paintbrush as close as possible to the time you will be serving the cake. A professional glazing product (available from cake-decorating suppliers) is a clear gel for glazing tortes and fruit.

STICKING ICING

Icing is made from sugar, so it will stick with the addition of water alone. You can use syrup (see page 42) instead of water if you prefer. Paint a very faint line of water on the fondant icing and stick the decorative icing shape on top. Don't apply too much water, or the icing will become soggy.

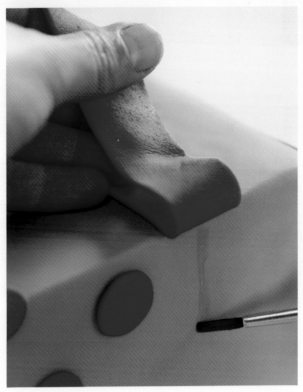

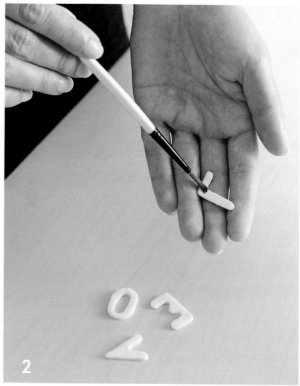

CUTTING AND PLACING SHAPES

1. CUT SHAPES FROM ROLLED ICING

Roll a thin sheet of icing about 3 mm (⅛ inch) thick, using a pasta machine or a rolling pin. Mark the position for the placement of the shapes on the cake using a pin or toothpick.

2. PAINT WITH WATER

You can use syrup (see page 42) instead of water if you prefer. Paint the back of the shape with water using a small paintbrush. Don't apply too much water, or the icing will become soggy.

3. APPLY TO CAKE

Gently press the shapes in place using your fingers. Don't push too hard or you will flatten the icing.

PLACING RIBBON

1. MEASURE THE CAKES

Use a flexible tape measure to check the lengths of ribbon required. Wrap the ribbon around the cake and adhere with double-sided tape. Place the join at the back of the cake or cover with a small neat bow.

2. MAKE A BOW

In narrow ribbon, simply tie a neat bow and trim the ends. Adhere to the cake with double-sided adhesive tape. To make a bow from wider ribbon, cut a length of ribbon double the length of the bow and turn it over so the wrong side is facing up. Stick some double-sided adhesive tape in the centre and fold each end over to adhere in the centre. Cut a short piece of ribbon to fold over the centre of the bow and secure it at the back with double-sided adhesive tape.

MAKING A TEMPLATE

Making templates is an essential part of cake decorating: once you master this skill you will be able to create your own unique decorations. Use a reference image such as a font or picture and trace it onto tracing paper. Cut out the shape and use it as a pattern for cutting or use a pin to prick dots into the icing around the outline.

TRACING

To transfer lettering or a design directly onto fondant icing, use tracing paper and a 2B pencil.

1. TRACE THE IMAGE

Trace the desired shape or word onto tracing paper using a 2B pencil. Turn the paper over and trace over the back of the same image.

2. TRANSFER TO ICING

Place the traced image right way up on the cake. By lightly shading over the pencil lines on the tracing paper you can transfer the image onto the cake.

BASIC PAINTING

I recommend using a fine paintbrush for cake painting. Mix a small amount of food colouring paste with cake decorator's alcohol and paint a test on a scrap of icing first. It is best to paint on white or light-coloured icing as painting on coloured icing means that you are actually mixing colour pigments and could end up with a colour you never intended. The 'paint' dries almost instantly, so work with small quantities at a time and work quickly.

PAINTING IN SILVER & GOLD

Purchase edible gold or silver paint from a cake-decorating supplier. Alternatively, nontoxic silver and gold dust can be found in nearly all cake-decorating suppliers. Mix the edible metallic dust with cake decorator's alcohol and then use a fine paintbrush to apply.

The silver and gold dust can spread everywhere and contaminate your cake and decorations. Place paper underneath the project when using the dust; if you are painting directly onto the cake, cover unpainted areas of the cake with paper before proceeding.

EDIBLE GLITTER

Nontoxic edible glitter is available from cake-decorating suppliers and is easy to apply. Trace the area you wish to cover with the glitter using a paintbrush and water or piping gel. Dust the wet area with the edible glitter and wait until it is dry, then remove any excess glitter with a soft paintbrush. Carefully tilt the cake to shake off any loose glitter.

CREATING YOUR OWN STENCIL

1. CHOOSE A DESIGN

Measure the part of the cake you want to create the stencil for. Reduce or enlarge the image for the stencil and print it out. Check that it will fit on the cake.

2. TAPE TO A BOARD

Tape the image onto a cutting board or mat, place a sheet of acetate film over the image and firmly tape it in place.

3. CUT OUT DESIGN

Using a craft knife, carefully cut through the plastic along the outlines of the design.

4. TRIM TO SIZE

Lift the acetate away from the template and cut away excess plastic around the edges if necessary. Place the stencil on the cake and secure with masking tape. Apply royal icing, edible paint or edible glitter, allow to dry, then carefully remove the stencil.

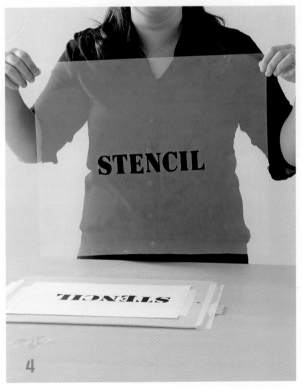

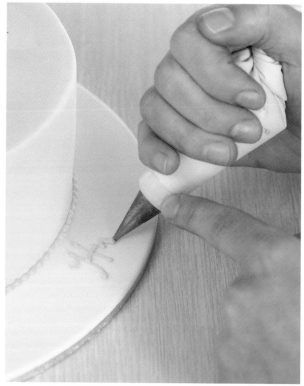

PIPING

It is much easier to pipe on firm icing, so cover the cake and leave it overnight.

The round piping tips used for royal icing come in an assortment of sizes: #00–#12 (the numbers correspond with the size of the opening, #00 being the smallest). A #1 piping tip and smaller could be frustrating for new decorators, so start with #2 tip or bigger and gradually work your way up to fine piping.

ROYAL ICING

You can make royal icing from scratch (see page 42) or buy instant royal icing, which is a good substitute. Before piping with royal icing, it is essential to have it at the correct consistency, not too runny but not too thick, or it will keep

blocking the piping tip and drive you crazy! Royal icing dries to a very hard consistency and it will begin setting as soon as it is made. It is very important to keep the icing covered when you are not using it! Store it in an airtight container.

COLOUR

If you wish to colour the royal icing, add food colouring paste in very small quantities and mix the royal icing and colour together using a palette knife. We do this on the work surface, but you may want to try a board or plate. Don't make the colour too dark, as it will darken when it dries.

To create longer messages you need to learn a 'font': your piping font will be as individual as you are and I can still recognise who made a cake years later just by the piping font on the board. Practise as much and as often as you can, on the side of a cake tin, on a sheet of baking paper or on the work surface. Practise with chocolate hazelnut spread or toothpaste as they are easy, cheap and always ready. Our trainees practise daily.

EQUIPMENT

At Planet Cake we make our piping bags from baking paper because we pipe all day long; however, fabric and disposable plastic icing bags are perfect for home decorating. Remember that if you have a fabric bag like the one pictured you will need a coupler as well as a piping tip.

FILLING THE BAG

Fill the piping bag one-third full with royal icing: make sure the icing is pushed down towards the piping end of the bag and give it a few squeezes to get rid of air pockets. If you find it difficult to hold the bag and fill it at the same time you can place the bag in a glass to hold it while you fill it.

PRACTICE

If you have never piped before then the best way to practise is to pipe some icing lines. Fit the piping bag with a piping tip and hold the bag with two hands (see photo): one hand to guide and the other to squeeze the bag. Hold the piping bag at a 45-degree angle just above the work surface and apply pressure. Watch the icing emerge from the tip. Secure the end of the icing thread to the surface then pipe along a line, allowing the thread to fall into position. Piping is an obvious choice when decorating a cake, but it is easy to be discouraged by complicated piping designs. Start with simple designs and practise until you are perfect.

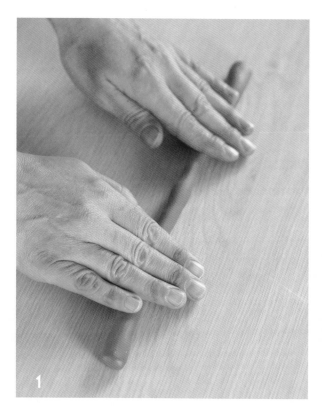 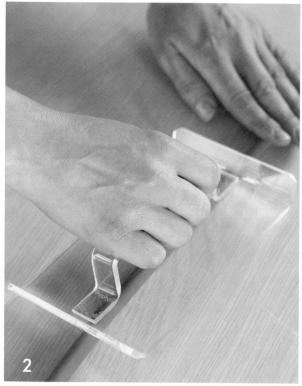

ICING ROLL (SAUSAGE)

To create and apply an even rope of icing, all you need is some fondant icing, a paintbrush, water, an icing smoother and a sharp knife.

1. ROLL A ROPE

Start by rolling the icing in your hands to create the basic elongated shape.

2. SMOOTH AND STRETCH

Set the roll on the work surface, and use an acrylic smoother to roll the rope back and forth, pulling slightly to the sides to elongate the rope. If the icing begins to slip under the smoother and does not roll easily, use a paintbrush to paint a thin line of water right next to and parallel to the rope, then use the smoother to roll the icing across the water. This will make the icing a little bit stickier, which will help it 'catch' and roll easily underneath the smoother. Continue to roll and stretch the icing rope until it is the desired width and length.

3. APPLY TO THE CAKE

Place the rope around the cake, using a dab of water to stick it if required. Where the ends meet, cut them flush and use a small ball of icing to cover the join: it will look like a little 'pearl'.

RUFFLES

1. MAKE FRILLED STRIPS

Colour the icing before you begin. Roll a piece of icing in a pasta machine to about 3 mm (⅛ inch) thick. Cut strips approximately 3 cm (1¼ inches) wide. Cover the strips with vinyl or plastic while you are not using them. Dust a strip with cornflour (cornstarch) underneath. Use a frilling tool on a petal pad, rolling the tool left and right to create a ruffled look. Work all the way along one edge of the icing strip.

2. APPLY TO THE CAKE

Mark lines on the cake to indicate the placement of each ruffle. Use a fine paintbrush to apply a little water to the cake and adhere the flat edge of the ruffle along the marked lines.

3. PRESS GENTLY

Use your fingers to press the ruffles gently onto the cake. Keep the joins at the back of the cake, staggering them slightly so they don't all line up exactly. Trim any excess length from the ruffles to allow the joins to sit flush.

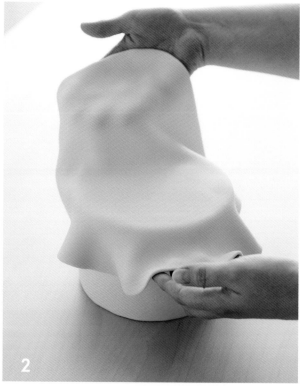

MAKING A LID

Let the covered cake sit for at least a couple of hours before you add the lid, in order for the icing to harden a little.

1. PREPARE THE ICING AND THE CAKE

Roll a piece of fondant icing larger than the cake. Use a paintbrush to lightly dab the cake with water where you would like the lid to sit.

2. PLACE THE ICING

Roll the icing onto a rolling pin, lift it up and unroll it over the cake.

3. SMOOTH

Smooth the top and sides with your hands or a flexiscraper.

4. MARK THE EDGE

Use a ruler to mark the lower edge of the lid. Make sure the lip of the lid is wide enough to cover the water line you have marked, or when you cut the icing it will be sloppy underneath.

5. TRIM OFF EXCESS

Trim the lid using a clean sharp paring knife. This is easiest when the cake is on a turntable.

MAKING A BOW

1. ROLL AND CUT ICING

Roll fondant icing to approximately 3 mm (⅛ inch) thick using a rolling pin or pasta machine. Cut two rectangles 13 x 25 cm (5 x 10 inches). Lay a vinyl sheet on top of the rectangle you are not working on so it does not dry out and crack. Using a small paintbrush, brush about 1 cm (⅜ inch) of the two short sides of the rectangle lightly with water.

2. MAKE PLEATS

Pinch pleats on both short sides of the rectangle simultaneously.

3. ADD PADDING

Place cotton wool in the middle of the rectangle.

4. FORM A LOOP

Bring both pleated sides together and gently press the pleated ends.

5. MAKE A FLAT BASE

Fold one side of the bow loop underneath to create a flat base that will sit on the cake.

6. MAKE A SECOND LOOP

Set the loop aside and repeat the process with the other icing rectangle to make the other half. Trim the centre and push the loops together.

7. CUT A CENTRE WRAP

Cut a small strip of the leftover icing and fold the short sides into pleats. Wrap the pleated strip around the bow centre and pinch the ends together at the back.

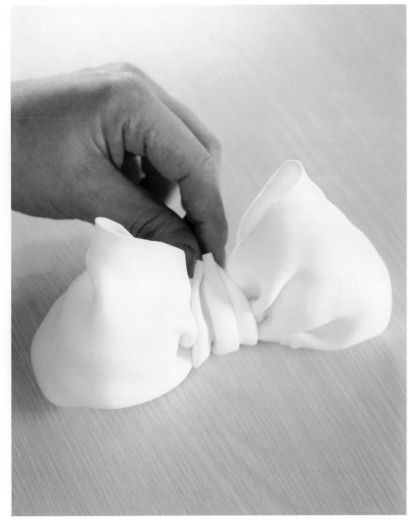

CUTTING &
APPLYING STRIPES

1. MEASURE THE CAKE

This task will be easier if you raise the cake slighlty from the work surface by standing it on a styrofoam block or turntable slightly smaller than the cake. Measure the length of the side or the circumference of the cake to work out how wide to make the stripes. Use the blade of a paring knife to gently mark the positions of the stripes on the icing.

2. CUT THE STRIPES

Roll out fondant icing to approximately 3 mm (⅛ inch) thick and cut stripes to the width you've calculated. You can create a template for the stripes from waxed cardboard, or simply cut them with a pizza cutter and ruler. Place the stripes you're not using under a vinyl sheet to keep them from drying out as you work.

3. ADHERE TO THE CAKE

Carefully brush from the base of the cake to the top with a little water along one of the marked lines.

4. APPLY THE STRIPES

Apply each icing stripe vertically from the top down, beginning with the top end flush with the top of the cake.

5. TRIM THE ICING

Trim off the excess icing stripe at the base with a clean knife.

6. CHECK FOR STRAIGHTNESS

Use the edge of a ruler to ensure that the stripe is straight. Smooth the stripes with a flexiscraper.

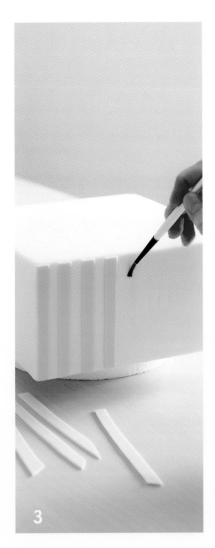

3

4

5

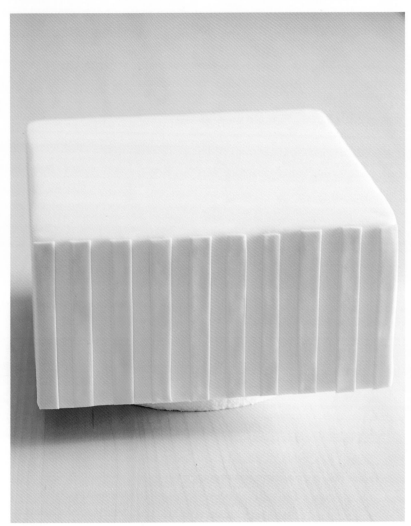

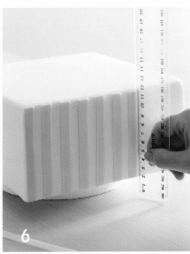

6

FRESH FLOWERS

Fresh flowers can be a beautiful classic statement for any occasion and they are a great replacement for sugar flowers if you don't want to, or don't have time to make them. I absolutely love fresh flower cakes, especially for outdoor weddings; let's face it, nothing can compare to the real thing. There are two ways to do this, either get the florist to dress the cake with flowers when they are dressing the venue, or you can do it yourself: it really is quite simple. The rule of thumb is that you must dress the cake with flowers as close as possible to the event time as you do not want the flowers to spoil or be affected by heat.

USING A FLORIST

If using a florist to dress your cake it is important to choose a person who has had experience in dressing cakes: we recommend asking to view some of their previous work to confirm that their style mirrors yours and sending them photos of your cake before they dress it so they are prepared. It is very important that you not only discuss the fresh flower cake with the florist but also with the venue. If a florist is going to dress a cake on site they will need time and space to move: restaurants and busy venues may not allow enough time to dress the cake, so make sure these details are confirmed.

DIY FRESH FLOWERS

CHOOSE FLOWERS

As a general rule, firm flowers, such as roses and orchids, work beautifully, while delicate flowers, such as gardenias, and flowers with long stems, such as arum lilies and tulips, can be difficult. Do some research and make sure that the flowers you choose will last the distance. Keep poisons off your cake! Certainly try to seek out flowers that have been organically grown so that no chemical or pesticide residue is transferred to the cake. Even edible flowers should not be eaten if they have been sprayed with pesticides.

PLACE FLOWERS

Never push the flower stems directly into the cake. You will need posy spikes that you can buy from any cake-decorating supplier.

1   Fill cake flower spikes with room-temperature water and put them in a bowl. Using scissors, cut single flower stems on a slant; the stems should be 5–7.5 cm (2–3 inches) long.

2   Insert each flower into a water-filled tube or spike.

3   Excess water may squirt out, so wipe the tube completely dry before inserting it into the cake. Flower petals can be scattered on the cake just before your guests see the display.

FIGURINES & FLOWERS

FIGURINES

TEDDY BEAR

By varying the colour of the icing and the shape of the face and ears you can use this technique to make many different animal figurines, including the cats on page 186.

MATERIALS

110 g (3¾ oz) brown ready-to-roll fondant icing
5 g (³⁄₁₆ oz) contrasting ready-to-roll fondant icing
tiny amount of black fondant icing
Tylose powder

1   Roll each of the coloured icing balls lightly in Tylose powder and knead it in until well combined. Return each ball to its resealable plastic bag until you are ready to use it.

BODY

2   Roll 50 g (1¾ oz) of brown icing into a smooth seamless ball between the palms of your hands, exerting a regular pressure. Shape into a pear shape.

LEGS

3   Starting with a ball of 5 g (³⁄₁₆ oz) of brown icing, roll a cylinder about 4 cm (1½ inches) long. Pinch one end with your index finger and thumb to make a foot shape. Make a second leg in the same way. Stick the legs onto the body with a dab of water.

ARMS

4   Starting with a ball of 5 g (³⁄₁₆ oz) of brown icing, roll a cylinder about 4 cm (1½ inches) long. Flatten one end of the arm at the front to make it look like a paw. Make a second arm with another 5 g of icing. Stick the arms to the body with a dab of water, curving them around the belly as in the pictures.

HEAD & FACE

5   Roll 35 g (1¼ oz) of brown icing into a seamless ball. Take icing in a contrasting colour and roll it into a marble-size flat oval. Press it onto the head and gently roll to fuse them together.

EARS

6   Roll a small ball of brown icing until smooth. Use a ball tool to indent the centre slightly. Roll a ball of about half the size in icing of a contrasting colour. Stick it into the indentation in the brown ball with a dab of water, and gently indent again. Cut in half with a paring knife. Bend each ear a little and stick them to the bear's head with a dab of water.

One day ahead, colour the icing as required, then roll each colour into a ball. Place each ball in its own resealable plastic bag so the icing doesn't dry out.

NOSE & EYES

7   Use a tiny ball of black icing to create a nose and adhere it to the face with a dab of water.

8   Use a frilling tool to make a smile. Mark indentation for the eyes.

9   Roll tiny balls of black icing and adhere in the eye indentations with a dab of water.

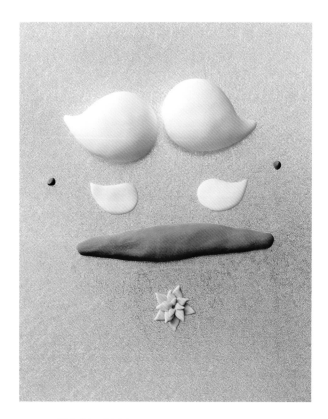

LOVE BIRDS

MATERIALS

60 g (2¼ oz) ready-to-roll fondant icing, for the body

10 g (¼ oz) ready-to-roll fondant icing, for the wings

tiny amounts of black, orange and purple fondant icing

40 g (1½ oz) ready-to-roll brown fondant icing

Tylose powder

toothpicks

One day ahead, colour the icing as required, then roll each colour into a ball. Place each ball in its own resealable plastic bag so the icing doesn't dry out.

1 Roll each of the coloured icing balls lightly in Tylose powder and knead it in until well combined. Return each ball to its resealable plastic bag until you are ready to use it.

BODY

2 To make the bodies, divide the body icing in half and roll two balls until there are no cracks. Shape them into rounded cone shapes. Press the shape gently on a hard bench to flatten the back of the bird. Turn the narrow end up slightly to form the tail, then press the base of the body on a hard bench to make a level base for the bird. Insert a skewer or toothpick about halfway up inside the body of each bird.

WINGS

3 To make the wings, roll the white icing out to approximately 2 mm (¹⁄₁₆ inch) thick and use a petal cutter to cut one wing for each bird. Use your fingers to slightly manipulate the tip of each wing so it turns upward. Allow to dry for 1–2 hours before assembling.

4 Cut 2 tiny triangles of orange icing and adhere them to the centre of each bird's face with a dab of water.

5 Make indents for the eyes using the point of a frilling tool or a toothpick. Roll 4 tiny balls of black icing for the eyes and adhere them in the indentations with a dab of water.

6 Use a dab of water to attach a wing to each bird.

BRANCH

7 Make a branch by rolling a fat sausage from the brown icing. Flatten it slightly and then taper the ends of the branch. Using the back of a knife or a frilling tool, scratch lines into the icing to create the appearance of a log.

8 While the brown icing is still soft, position the branch on top of the cake, then place the bodies of the birds, sticking the skewers right through the branch and into the cake. Trim the length of the skewers so that they don't hit bottom when you push them into the cake.

9 Make a flower by rolling the purple icing out approximately 3 mm (⅛ inch) thick and cutting a small disc using the wide end of a piping nozzle or a small circle cutter. Use your fingers to pinch out 13 triangular petals and apply the petals to the disc of icing with dabs of water. Make the outer and middle layer with five petals each and four petals for the top layer. Use water or piping gel to adhere the finished flower to the branch between the love birds.

OWLET

MATERIALS

80 g (2¾ oz) ready-to-roll fondant icing, coloured blue

20 g (¾ oz) ready-to-roll fondant icing, coloured pink

tiny amounts of brown, white, yellow and black
    fondant icing

Tylose powder

large heart cutter

barbecue skewer

One day ahead, colour the icing as required, then roll each colour into a ball. Place each ball in its own resealable plastic bag so the icing doesn't dry out.

1 Roll each of the coloured icing balls lightly in Tylose powder and knead it in until well combined. Return each ball to its resealable plastic bag until you are ready to use it.

BODY

2 To make the body roll the blue icing into a ball until there are no cracks and then shape it into an oval shape. Press the body gently on a hard bench to flatten the base. Use your fingertips to lightly pinch each side of the top of the head to create the 'ears' and press with a fingertip to hollow out the space between them. Allow to dry for an hour or two before assembling.

WINGS

3 To make the wings, roll out the pink icing thinly and use a large heart cutter to cut the shape.

Cut the heart shape in half vertically and turn the halves upside down to form the wings. Cup each wing in your hand and use a dab of water to adhere it to the side of the owl's body, smoothing it flat.

FEET & FACE

4 Roll small sausages of brown icing for the feet. Use a knife to indent the toes and adhere the feet to the front of the owl's body between the wings with a dab of water.

5 Roll out a tiny amount of white icing thinly and use the wide end of a piping tip or a small round cutter to cut two circles for the eyes. Adhere them to the owl's face with a dab of water.

6 Cut a small triangle of yellow icing to make a flat beak or model a small cone and adhere it with water just between the eye circles.

7 Make sure you take your time with the positioning of the pupils: too close together or too far apart and the owl will look a bit crazy. If you are nervous, lightly indent the pupils' positions with a toothpick to make sure you're happy with them. Roll tiny balls of black icing and press them into the indents.

8 A barbecue skewer will give extra support to the figurine once it's on the cake (this is a good idea if you are transporting the cake to a venue). While the owl is still soft, insert the skewer halfway up into the centre of the figurine and allow the figurine to dry overnight. Before placing the figurine, trim off any excess length from the skewer so that it won't hit bottom when you insert it into the cake.

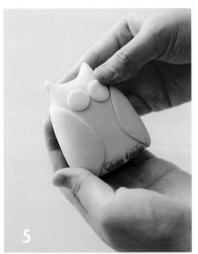

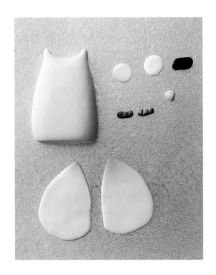

BABY BIRD

MATERIALS

40 g (1½ oz) ready-to-roll fondant
   icing, coloured yellow
tiny amounts of orange and black
   fondant icing
50 g (1¾ oz) ready-to-roll fondant
   icing, coloured brown
Tylose powder
toothpick

*One day ahead, colour the icing as required, then roll each colour into
a ball. Place each ball in its own resealable plastic bag so the icing
doesn't dry out.*

1 Roll each of the coloured icing balls lightly in Tylose powder
   and knead it in until well combined. Return each ball to its own
   resealable plastic bag until you are ready to use it.

BODY

2 To make the body, roll just less than half the yellow icing into a
   ball until there are no cracks and then shape it into an egg shape.
   Turn the narrow end of the egg slightly up and press the body
   gently on a hard work surface to slightly flatten the base.

HEAD

3 To make the head, set aside two small pieces of yellow icing for
   the wings and the head feathers and roll the remaining icing into
   a perfect ball with no cracks. Use a shortened toothpick to secure
   the head onto the body, or a piece of dry spaghetti can be used if
   you think that a child might eat the bird!

WINGS

4 To make the wings, roll two very small balls of icing and flatten
   them between your fingers. Mould into wing shapes by pinching
   the end and smoothing with your fingers. Allow to dry slightly
   before adhering to the sides of the body with a dab of water.

BEAK AND FEATHERS

5   Meanwhile, roll a small ball of orange icing for the beak into a cone shape and adhere with a dab of water. To create the head feathers, roll two very small balls of yellow icing into little sausages tapered at the ends. Use a frilling tool to poke tiny indents at the top of the head and delicately stick the thin end of each sausage into a hole with a dab of water.

EYES

6   The position of the eyes is all-important; they should be in the middle of the head, not too high up. Mark the position of the eyes with the point of a frilling tool or a toothpick before adhering them. Roll two minute black icing balls for the eyes and adhere with a dab of water.

NEST

7   To make the nest, roll out the brown icing in a very thin strip that is long enough to twist around the body of the bird. Use a knife or pizza cutter to cut thin strips of icing. Gather the strips gently into a bundle and twist them together slightly. Join them delicately at the back by interweaving the ends, making sure the nest will fit snugly around the baby bird.

8   Place the baby bird into the nest while the nest is still soft and allow them to dry together. Once they are completely dry, carefully transfer the nest and baby bird to the cake.

PEAS IN A POD

MATERIALS

40 g (1½ oz) ready-to-roll fondant icing, coloured pink

30 g (1 oz) ready-to-roll fondant icing, coloured green

tiny amount of black fondant icing

Tylose powder

toothpick

One day ahead, colour the icing as required, then roll each colour into a ball. Place each ball in its own resealable plastic bag so the icing doesn't dry out.

1   Roll each of the coloured icing balls lightly in Tylose powder and knead it in until well combined. Return each ball to its resealable plastic bag until you are ready to use it.

2   Divide the pink fondant icing into two balls of equal size and roll until there are no cracks.

3   Roll out the green fondant icing thinly with a small rolling pin and use a circle cutter to cut a circle large enough to wrap around the peas. Place the peas in the centre of the circle and fold it up on each side. Pinch the ends of the pod together and then squeeze it slightly in the middle.

4   Press the wide end of a piping tip lightly into each pea to create a smile, then using the point of the piping tip make a dimple at each end of the smiles.

5   Make two indents for the eyes and roll some very small balls of black icing to place in them.

6   Adhere the pea pod to the cake top with a little piping gel or a dab of water.

7   Use the leftover green fondant icing to make vines: roll multiple small balls into very thin little sausages using your fingers. Alternatively, use a pasta machine to create fine spaghetti-like strands. Wrap each strand lightly around a toothpick to form a curly tendril.

8   Ease the toothpick out of the curl and adhere the vines to the pea pod with a dab of water.

ROSE

MATERIALS

1 piece 18-gauge white wire

2.5 cm (1 inch) styrofoam ball

1 quantity flower paste (see page 43)

1 quantity piping gel

sugar glue

15 short pieces 28-gauge wire, each about 5 cm
   (2 inches) long

florists' stem tape

petal dust

EQUIPMENT

wire cutters

hot-glue gun and glue sticks

pasta machine

rose petal cutters (four graduating sizes)

vinyl sheet

ball tool and petal pad

apple tray

paintbrush

bamboo skewer

dental floss

1   Use hot glue to fix the end of the wire into the styrofoam ball.

2   You will use only the four largest sizes from a petal cutter set. Roll the flower paste by hand or in a pasta machine to 1–1.5 mm (1/32–1/16 inch) thick. Using the smaller of the four petal cutters, cut nine petals. Keep the petals and flower paste covered with a vinyl sheet when you are not working with them.

3   Use the ball tool to shape the edges of two of the petals. Apply piping gel to the styrofoam ball and stick the two petals on. It's okay to leave a little styrofoam exposed at this stage.

4   Take three more petals and use the ball tool to thin the edges by rolling around the curved end, and shape the edges. Apply sugar glue and stick the three petals onto the rose, over the two preceding petals.

5   Take the remaining small petals and repeat step 3. Remember to keep the centre of the rose tight.

6   Using the next size of petal cutter, cut four more petals from the flower paste sheet. Thin and ball the curved edges of the petals and dry them in an apple tray until they are leathery. Brush the point at the base of the petals with sugar glue using a paintbrush.

7   Apply these petals to the rose, making sure they are looser than the previous petals. Hang the rose upside down to dry.

8   Using the third petal cutter, cut four more petals from the flower paste sheet. Thin and ball the curved edges as before, then curl the top of each rose petal by rolling the edge over a toothpick.

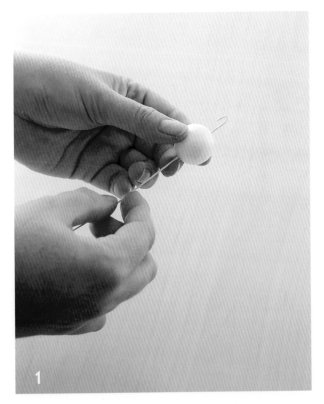

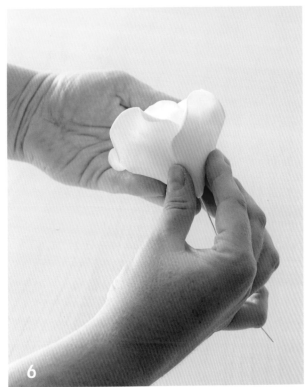

9   Dry the petals on an apple tray until they are leathery.

10 Brush the point of each petal with sugar glue and stick the petals on the rose with the rolled edges on the outside, overlapping the petals. Scrunch a piece of foil into a cup shape to hold the rose petals in position while the flower is drying overnight.

11 Meanwhile, cut seven more petals using the third petal cutter. Thin and ball the curved edges using a ball tool. Insert a short length of 28-gauge wire (about 5 cm/2 inches long) into the point of each petal. Curl the upper edges of the petals with a bamboo skewer, as before, and dry over an upturned apple tray.

12 Cut eight petals using the largest petal cutter. Thin and ball the curved edges using a ball tool. Insert a short length of 28-gauge wire (about 5 cm/2 inches long) into the point of each petal. Curl the upper edges of the petals with a bamboo skewer, as before, and dry over an upturned apple tray.

13 The next day, when all the petals are dry, use a length of dental floss and bind the seven smaller petals around the rose in an overlapping fashion. Repeat this step with the eight larger petals.

14 Bind the stem of the rose with florists' stem tape and trim the wires. Dust the centre of the flower with petal dust.

ROSE LEAVES

MATERIALS

1 quantity flower paste (see page 43)
1 length 26-gauge white wire
food colouring paste
petal dust (optional)
cooking oil spray (optional)

EQUIPMENT

small acrylic rolling pin
pasta machine
rose leaf cutter
vinyl sheet
ball tool and petal pad
leaf veiners
paintbrush

1   Roll a small amount of flower paste into a rectangle on a board or work surface and then roll it through a pasta machine, until it is about 1–1.5 mm ($\frac{1}{32}$–$\frac{1}{16}$ inch) thick. Cut out leaves with the cutter and cover them with a vinyl sheet to avoid drying out.

2   Working with one leaf at a time, insert the moistened end of a length of 26-gauge wire approximately half way into leaf from the stem end. Add veins to each leaf by placing it in a leaf veiner.

3   Thin the leaf edges using a ball tool on a petal pad. Twist the leaf a little to make it look natural, but don't twist it too much or they will be too difficult to arrange into the spray.

4   Paint the leaves using food colouring paste. Use petal dust to add depth of colour if you wish. If you want glossy leaves, they can be lightly sprayed with cooking oil spray.

Be careful when deciding exactly where you will put the flowers on the cake. If you place a sugar flower incorrectly, when you move it there will be a big hole. The petals are extremely fragile and I would advise making a hole using a skewer first if the icing is hard, then place the sugar flower using a pair of long tweezers to assist you in getting the flower wire into the hole without having to touch the petals. If the petals break, your heart will break as well after so much hard work!

Make the sugar paste flowers well in advance. They will keep for weeks in a cool, dry place.

PEONY & LEAVES

MATERIALS

1 length 18-gauge white wire

2.5 cm (1 inch) styrofoam ball

1 quantity flower paste (see page 43)

food colouring paste

piping gel

short lengths of 26-gauge wire

1 bunch fine flower stamens

florists' stem tape

petal dust

EQUIPMENT

hot glue gun and glue sticks

small acrylic rolling pin

pasta machine

peony petal and leaf cutters

vinyl sheet

ball tool and petal pad

peony flower veiner

apple tray

flat-edge paintbrush

CLOSED PEONY BUD

1   Use hot glue to fix the end of the wire into the styrofoam ball.

2   Colour the flower paste if desired using food colouring paste.
    Roll the flower paste by hand or in a pasta machine to 1–1.5 mm
    (1/32–1/16 inch) thick. On a nonstick surface, cut six petals using
    the smallest peony petal cutter. Keep the petals and flower paste
    covered with a vinyl sheet when you are not working with them.

3   Use the ball tool to thin out and shape the curved edge of each
    of the petals, putting gentle, consistent pressure with the ball
    half on and half off the edge of the petal.

4   Apply piping gel to the styrofoam ball and stick three of the
    petals on, tucking the second petal under the edge of the
    first, the third under the second. Ensure that you can't see the
    styrofoam ball when you have applied all of the petals. Apply the
    remaining petals in a second layer in the same way as the first
    and set the completed bud aside to dry.

OPEN PEONY WITH STAMENS

1 Slip a length of 26-gauge wire under the bunch of stamens and bind in the centre by twisting the wire around. Bend the stamens upwards in the middle.

2 Use white florists' stem tape to tape over the wire and then fan out the stamens for a loose, messy look.

PEONY PETALS

1 Using a pasta machine, roll out the petal paste to an even thickness, approximately 1–1.5 mm (1/32–1/16 inch).

2 For the first layer of petals, using the smallest of the set of three peony petal cutters, cut five petals. Insert a length of 26-gauge wire, approximately one-third of the way into the petal from the pointy end. Gently pinch the point with your fingers to secure the wire. Press the petal veiner over each petal.

3 Use the ball tool to thin and shape the curved edge of each petal as you did for the bud, at left. Curl the petals slightly and then place them inside the hollows of an apple tray to mould the curve. Allow the petals to dry completely overnight.

4 Repeat steps 2 and 3 using the second peony petal cutter to cut five medium petals.

5 Repeat steps 2 and 3 using the largest peony petal cutter to cut five large petals.

COLOURING

1 Starting with a soft pink colour for the flower paste, you can add depth of colour beginning from the base of the petal up, using petal dust. Apply petal dust with a dry paintbrush, as you would apply blusher to your cheeks.

2 Hold the petal upside down by the wire, and apply petal dust using a flat-edge paintbrush with a downward motion, so the deeper colour is applied at the base and gets lighter towards the tip of the petal.

3 Dust the stamen centre with yellow petal dust or paint with food colouring paste mixed with cake decorator's alcohol.

ASSEMBLY

1 Assemble the smallest petals very tightly at the base of the stamen centre. Use florists' stem tape to secure the wires together, using your fingers to push the tape right up to the wire.

2 Gradually add the next layer of medium-size petals, securing each one firmly with tape at the base of the first layer.

3 Repeat with the largest petals, and bind with tape right down the length of wire.

4 Adjust the position of the petals if necessary, so that they are closer around the centre and more open as the flower gets larger.

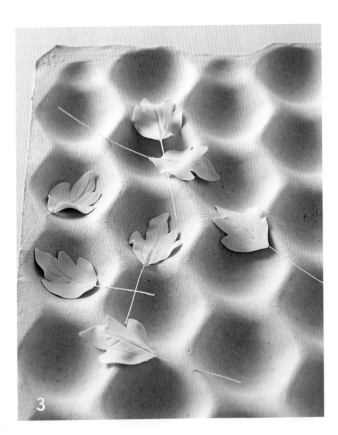

PEONY LEAVES

1   Colour the remaining flower paste green. Using a pasta machine, roll out the green flower paste to an even thickness, approximately 1–1.5 mm ($\frac{1}{32}$–$\frac{1}{16}$ inch).

2   Using the peony leaf cutter, cut at least nine peony leaves. Insert a length of 26-gauge wire, approximately one-third of the way into the leaf from the stem end. Gently pinch the point with your fingers to secure the wire. Press the leaf veiner over each leaf.

3   Use the ball tool to thin and shape the edges of each leaf. Lay some of the leaves over the mounds of an apple tray, and stand some upright by pushing the wires into a styrofoam block. Allow the leaves to dry completely overnight.

4   Using florists' stem tape to secure the wires, arrange the leaves in groups of two and three, to assemble in your arrangement.

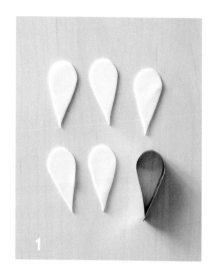

FRANGIPANIS

MATERIALS

1 quantity flower paste
   (see page 43)
short lengths of 24-gauge wire
   (optional)
petal dust

EQUIPMENT

small acrylic rolling pin
pasta machine
frangipani petal cutter
vinyl sheet
ball tool and petal pad
paintbrush

1   Using a pasta machine, roll out the flower paste to an even thickness, approximately 1–1.5 mm ($\frac{1}{32}$–$\frac{1}{16}$ inch). Cut out five petals for each flower using a frangipani petal cutter. Keep the petals and flower paste covered with a vinyl sheet when you are not working with them.

2   Use a ball tool on a petal pad to thin the curved edges, and curl the left side, of each petal slightly.

3   Moisten the right edge of one petal and lay another petal on top, overlapping by about one-third. Repeat the process with the remaining petals, forming a fan shape.

4   Quickly roll the flower into shape, overlapping the first petal with the last, and squeeze the base of the flower slightly to firm it up. If the flowers are to be wired, insert a short length of 24-gauge wire.

5   Stand the wired flowers in an upside-down egg carton with holes punched in the cups and use a paint brush to gently ease the petals open. Allow to dry overnight.

6   Using a soft paintbrush, colour the centre of the flower with pink or yellow petal dust.

CAKE DECORATING IDEAS

CUPCAKES

If you have never decorated a cake before, then cupcakes
are a fantastic place to start. Cupcakes will introduce you
to most of the equipment and materials that you will
use for bigger cakes and will allow you to practise the
techniques on a smaller scale. Cupcakes are also great
for smaller celebrations; however, I must caution you
that making more than 50 can often become even more
time-consuming than making a bigger cake. Cupcakes also
only last four days when covered with rolled fondant icing,
so you have less decorating time than you do with a larger
cake. These simple cupcake designs would be appropriate
for all of the celebrations covered in this book, so play
around with them and adjust the colours as you wish.
Cupcakes always make a big impact!

CUPCAKES

MATERIALS

20–30 g (¾–1 oz) ganache
   per cupcake
20–30 g (¾–1 oz) ready-to-roll
   fondant icing per cupcake,
   coloured
small amounts of ready-to-roll
   fondant icing, extra,
   for decorations
food colouring paste
royal icing
gold edible paint, for 'love' and
   tiny hearts cupcakes
silver cachous, for quilted cupcake

EQUIPMENT

ganaching tools
icing tools
pasta machine
rolling pins, small and large
piping (icing) bag and #1 nozzle
paintbrush
stitching tool
frilling tool
baking paper
2B pencil
waxed cardboard
paring knife
flower plunger cutter

Ganache the cupcakes (see page 47) and cover them with fondant icing (see page 56). Leave overnight to set.

BOW

1 Roll a small amount of fondant icing in the pasta machine until it is approximately 3 mm (⅛ inch) thick. Cut the icing into 1.5 cm (⅝ inch) strips: then cut two 3 cm (1¼ inch) pieces with one end cut at an angle; cut two 5 cm (2 inch) pieces for the bow loops; and cut one 1.5 cm (⅝ inch) piece for the centre of the bow.

2 Fold one of the 5 cm pieces in half to form a bow loop.

3 Pleat the joined ends together.

4 Pleat the flat ends of the 3 cm pieces and use a little water to stick them on the cupcake in a V shape to form the ribbon tails. Stick the bow loops in place over the point of the V.

5 Finish the bow by wrapping the short piece of icing over the centre between the loops.

LOVE

1 Make sure the icing has set so that it is firm enough to pipe on. Make a batch of white royal icing (see page 42) and fill a piping (icing) bag fitted with a #1 piping tip.

2 Trace or copy the lettering onto the icing following the instructions on page 78, or work freehand if you are confident.

3 Following the general advice on piping (see page 82), pipe the royal icing over the lettering. Allow to dry.

4 When the piped icing is dry, use gold edible paint to paint the letters, or mix a small amount of edible gold lustre dust with cake decorator's alcohol and apply it to the letters using a fine paintbrush.

TINY HEARTS

1   Make sure the icing has set so that it is firm enough to pipe on. Make a batch of white royal icing (see page 42) and fill a piping (icing) bag fitted with a #1 piping tip.

2   Following the general advice on piping (see page 82), pipe the royal icing to make little hearts. The hearts are created by placing two teardrops side by side with points touching.

3   When the royal icing is dry, use gold edible paint to paint the hearts, or mix a small amount of edible gold lustre dust with cake decorator's alcohol and apply it to the hearts using a fine paintbrush.

QUILTED CUPCAKE

1   While the icing is still soft use the back of a knife or the edge of a ruler to mark a cross through the centre point of the cupcake. Add two more lines evenly spaced on each side of the arms of the cross to form the quilt pattern.

2   Run a stitching tool along the marked lines.

3   Use the tip of a paintbrush handle or a frilling tool to make indentations where the lines cross.

4   Push a silver cachou into each indentation.

ROLLED ROSE

1 Make sure the icing has set so that it is firm enough to pipe on. Make a batch of white royal icing (see page 42) and fill a piping (icing) bag fitted with a #1 piping tip.

2 Following the general advice on piping (see page 82), pipe the royal icing in straight lines radiating out from the centre of the cupcake.

3 Roll a small amount of fondant icing in the pasta machine until it is approximately 3 mm (⅛ inch) thick. Cut the icing into a 3 cm (1¼ inch) wide strip and trim the ends square. Cut the strip into 8 cm (3¼ inch) lengths and keep them covered until ready to use.

4 Take one strip at a time and start rolling it, slightly folding the top edge outwards as you roll to create a petal effect.

5 Pinch the rose at the base and cut off any excess icing.

6 Stick the rose in the centre of the iced cupcake, using a dab of water.

A BIRDIE TOLD ME

1 Make sure the cupcake icing has set. Make a template of a bird from waxed cardboard. Colour a small amount of fondant icing for the wings (or use scraps left over from icing the cupcakes).

2 Roll a small amount of fondant icing in the pasta machine until it is approximately 3 mm (⅛ inch) thick. Use the template and a sharp paring knife to cut out the bird shape. If you are confident, you can cut out the bird shape freehand.

3 Place the bird shape on the cupcake using a small dab of water applied with a paintbrush to stick it down. Repeat steps 2 and 3 to cut and place the bird's wings.

4 Make a batch of white royal icing (see page 42) and put it into a piping (icing) bag fitted with a #1 piping tip. Following the general advice on piping (see page 82), pipe legs for the bird in the royal icing.

DAISY

1 Make sure the cupcake icing has set. Roll a small amount of white fondant icing in the pasta machine until it is approximately 3 mm (⅛ inch) thick. Use a flower plunger cutter to cut out one flower for each cupcake.

2 Press the end of a frilling tool into each petal.

3 Carefully transfer the daisy to the cupcake, placing it off-centre. Use your finger to slightly curl up the end of each petal.

4 Roll a small ball of yellow fondant icing and adhere in the centre of the daisy with a tiny dab of water.

FRIENDSHIP CAKES

It is often challenging to find ways to show friends how much you care about them, especially if you are on a limited budget; however, cakes send the perfect message. Not only are they a fantastic gift but, because you have made it yourself, it says exactly what you want it to say. Think about it this way: I am sure you would struggle to remember a lot of the presents you have received over the years, but I am certain that, like me, you can remember almost every cake someone has baked for you. My advice would be to do your research early: find out your friend's favourite cake flavour, colour or hobby. Planning ahead will ensure an awesome cake!

YOU'RE SO SWEET

Don't be daunted by this sweet cake, it is easier than it looks. If you've got time to spare, make as many sweets as you like and pile them on top of the cake.

MATERIALS

20 cm (8 inch) round cake

syrup

800 g (1 lb 12 oz) ganache

20 cm (8 inch) round cake board

30 cm (12 inch) round display board (optional)

1 kg (2 lb 4 oz) ready-to-roll white fondant icing

850 g (1 lb 14 oz) ready-to-roll fondant icing, for display board (optional)

250 g (9 oz) ready-to-roll pink fondant icing, extra, for drips

250 g (9 oz) ready-to-roll fondant icing, extra, for decorations

food colouring paste

2 lollipop sticks

coloured sprinkles

EQUIPMENT

ganaching tools

icing tools

pasta machine (optional)

pizza cutter

paring knife

vinyl sheet

medium paintbrush

heart cutter, square cutter, small circle cutter

red edible ink marker

1   Follow the general instructions on how to ganache and prepare round cakes (see page 48). Allow to set overnight.

2   Cover the cake with white fondant icing, following the general instructions on how to cover round cakes (see page 54). Allow to set overnight.

3   If using a covered display board, use the extra fondant icing to cover the board following the general instructions on how to cover display boards (see page 58). Allow to set overnight.

4   Carefully transfer the cake to the display stand or the covered display board.

5   Roll out the pink fondant icing for the dripping icing layer until it is around 3 mm (⅛ inch) thick. The icing should be about 35 cm (14 inches) diameter. Using a pizza cutter, cut out a large uneven shape to create the overhanging dripping icing. Brush the top of the cake with a little water and place the dripping icing layer on top. Smooth it out and adjust the drips by cutting with a paring knife where necessary. Stick the drips down with dabs of water.

LOLLIPOPS

6 Roll two strips of icing, one coloured and one white.

7 Place the two rolls next to each other and start rolling them into a spiral from one end.

8 Flatten the ends of the rolls together and press them to the spiral to complete the lollipop. Push a lollipop stick into the lollipop at the point where the ends join.

HEARTS

9 Roll out small amounts of fondant icing approximately 3 mm (⅛ inch) thick and use a small heart cutter to cut out the hearts.

10 Use a red edible ink marker to write short messages on the hearts.

LICORICE ALLSORTS

11 Roll out small amounts of black and coloured fondant icing approximately 3 mm (⅛ inch) thick and cut small squares with a cutter.

12 Brush the surface of a black square with water and assemble layers with a dab of water on each, ending with a black square on top.

FINISHING

13 To make freckles (chocolate nonpareils), use a small circle cutter to cut circles of brown fondant and apply water to the surface. Cover with coloured sprinkles.

14 To make licorice logs, roll a long sausage of white fondant icing. Roll out some black icing approximately 3 mm (⅛ inch) thick and wrap it over the white fondant sausage. Trim off excess black icing and cut the log into short lengths, approximately 3–4 cm (1¼–1½ inches) long.

15 Insert the lollipop sticks into the centre of the cake and pile up the other sweets around the top of the cake.

GOOD LUCK

Whenever I work with glitter I sparkle for the rest of the day, which can be quite nice if you don't have anywhere important to go! I have chosen a square cake for this Chinese character–inspired design; however, red icing can be quite tricky if you are a beginner. This is a dead simple cake design: it works with any simple image and any cake shape. A round white cake would look equally good and you can change the glitter colour as you like. If you don't want to use the 'good luck' character shown here, simple motifs such as hearts or letters look great as well.

MATERIALS

18 cm (7 inch) square cake
syrup
830 g (1 lb 13 oz) ganache
18 cm (7 inch) square cake board
23 cm (9 inch) square cake display board (optional)
1 kg (2 lb 4 oz) ready-to-roll red fondant icing
650 g (1 lb 7 oz) ready-to-roll fondant icing, extra, for display board (optional)
piping gel
edible gold glitter
72 cm (28 inches) narrow red satin ribbon (optional)

EQUIPMENT

ganaching tools
icing tools
printed motif or symbol
scissors
baking paper
pastry brush
2 medium paintbrushes
fine paintbrush

1 Ganache the cake, following the general instructions on how to ganache and prepare square cakes (see page 50). Allow to set overnight.

2 We recommend using ready-made red fondant icing, rather than attempting to colour it yourself. Cover the cake with the fondant icing, following the general instructions on how to cover square cakes (see page 57). Allow to set overnight.

3 If using a covered display board, use the extra fondant icing to cover the board following the general instructions on how to cover display boards (see page 58). Allow to set overnight.

GLITTER MOTIF

4 Cut out the printed image and make sure it fits the cake. Lay a piece of baking paper on the work surface, place the image face down on the paper and use a pastry brush to paint the wrong side of the cut-out with piping gel.

5 With the cake on clean baking paper or a temporary cake board, carefully position the image, sticky side down, on the cake.

6 Lift off the paper cut-out and use a paintbrush to ensure that the piping gel covers all of the area that you want replicated.

7 Pour edible glitter over the top of the image, being quite liberal to make sure the whole motif is completely covered.

8 Tilt the cake carefully onto its side and allow the loose glitter to fall onto the baking paper. This is the messy part!

9 With the cake flat, use a dry paintbrush to dust away any loose glitter that remains on top of the cake. Tidy up the edges and allow the piping gel to dry completely.

10 Transfer the cake to the cake stand or the covered display board. If you wish, apply narrow red ribbon around the base of the cake, following the general instructions on page 77.

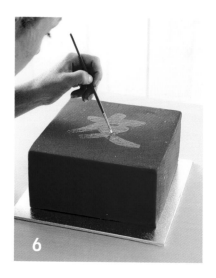

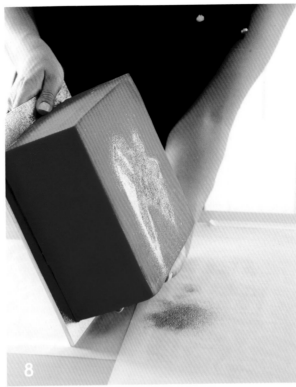

TWO PEAS IN A POD

This is a cake for best friends or to celebrate a relationship with a unique and special bond. Of course, this cake would also be perfect to celebrate the arrival of twins. This is a very sweet design in pastels but you could alter the mood with your colour choice; for example, red and white would look cheerful and festive. It's a design that's really flexible and making the figurines is also easy and fun.

If you don't feel confident with piping then make a round cake and just decorate it with confetti dots.

MATERIALS

15 cm (6 inch) square cake

syrup

655 g (1 lb 7 oz) ganache

15 cm (6 inch) square cake board

20 cm (8 inch) square cake display board (optional)

850 g (1 lb 14 oz) ready-to-roll fondant icing

550 g (1 lb 4 oz) ready-to-roll fondant icing, extra, for display board (optional)

cornflour (cornstarch)

two peas in a pod figurine (see page 105)

30 g (1 oz) ready-to-roll fondant icing, extra, for confetti dots

food colouring paste, various colours

water or piping gel

royal icing, coloured pale green

EQUIPMENT

ganaching tools

icing tools

paring knife

small rolling pin

piping (icing) bag and #1 or #2 piping tip

toothpicks

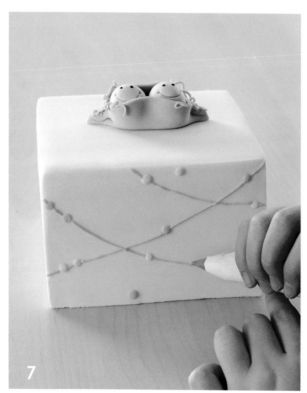

1 Ganache the cake, following the general instructions on how to ganache and prepare square cakes (see page 50). Allow to set overnight.

2 Cover the cake with the fondant icing, following the general instructions on how to cover square cakes (see page 57). Allow to set overnight.

3 If you are using a display board, cover it with the fondant icing, following the general instructions on how to cover display boards (see page 58). Allow to set overnight.

DECORATIONS

4 Make the two peas in a pod figurine, following the instructions on page 105. Place it carefully on top of the cake and arrange the tendrils gently around it.

5 Use a toothpick to lightly draw the lines for the streamers onto the sides of the cake.

6 Colour some small balls of fondant icing using tiny amounts of food colouring paste to keep the colours light. Pinch off even smaller pieces, roll into balls and squash them flat to create the confetti. Use a dab of water or piping gel to secure the confetti at intervals along the marked streamer lines.

7 Fill a piping (icing) bag with the royal icing following the general instructions on page 82. Pipe along the marked lines between the confetti dots. Don't worry if you make a mistake in your piping; just put another piece of confetti over it!

8 Allow the decorations to dry, then transfer the cake to a display stand or covered cake display board.

If you have a pasta machine, a clay extruder or any implement that will produce a thin spaghetti strand, you can create the streamers without piping.

ENGAGEMENT CAKES

This is quite possibly the most exciting time for any couple: they will be keen to share their joyous news with just about anyone who will listen. Whether they are having an engagement party or just a quiet family celebration, a cake is a must. It will never be forgotten. The soon-to-be-married couple may even enjoy making their own cake. Most of the engagement cakes we make at Planet Cake are fairly fun, as most couples don't want their cake to look like a wedding cake, but would rather it reflect their personalities or the way they met. The cake designs I have included in this chapter are all fun or classic and simple styles.

PRETTY RUFFLES

Ruffles, ruffles and more ruffles. On a smaller cake they give a touch of glamour and lightness without too much hard work. The ruffles on this cake are in ombre tones, which means dark to light shades of the same colour, and if you have the time to do this it looks fantastic.

MATERIALS

peony flower (see page 112)
20 cm (8 inch) round cake
syrup
800 g (1 lb 12 oz) ganache
20 cm (8 inch) round cake board
25 cm (10 inch) round cake display
   board (optional)
1.5 kg (3 lb 5 oz) ready-to-roll
   fondant icing
650 g (1 lb 7 oz) ready-to-roll
   fondant icing, extra, for display
   board (optional)
food colouring paste
cornflour (cornstarch), for dusting
75 cm (29 inches) of 12 mm
   (½ inch) wide satin ribbon in
   a colour to match the ruffles

EQUIPMENT

ganaching tools
icing tools
paring knife
pizza cutter
pastry brush
acrylic spacers
medium-size paintbrush
cornflour shaker
pasta machine (optional)
frilling tool
tape measure
scissors
ruler
turntable

1   Make the peony, following the instructions on page 112. Allow to dry for at least 24 hours.

2   Ganache the cake, following the general instructions on how to ganache and prepare round cakes (see page 48). Allow to set overnight.

3   Set aside 500 g (1 lb 2 oz) of the fondant icing for the ruffles. Cover the cake with the white fondant icing, following the general instructions on how to cover round cakes (see page 54). Allow to set overnight.

4   If you are using a display board, cover it with the extra fondant icing, following the general instructions on how to cover cake boards (see page 58). Allow to set overnight.

5   Transfer the cake to the display stand or covered display board.

RUFFLES

6 Using the remaining 500 g (1 lb 2 oz) of fondant, follow the instructions on how to colour fondant icing (see page 72). Colour the icing a very pale shade of your chosen colour using food colouring paste, then divide the icing into quarters and set one quarter aside. Add more of the food colouring paste to colour the remaining icing a slightly darker shade, then divide into thirds and set one aside; add more food colouring paste to colour the remainder a medium-dark shade and divide in half, setting half aside; finally add more food colouring paste to colour the remaining icing the darkest shade.

7 Follow the instructions for making ruffles (see page 85). Make two strips long enough to go right around the cake from each colour.

8 Stand the cake and its display board or stand on a turntable to make the next part easier. Scribe a line for the placement of the top layer of ruffles on the side of the cake, using acrylic spacers and a pin. Use a paintbrush to brush a line of water just above the scribed line.

9 Stick one of the lightest coloured strips on to the cake along the water line, making sure the ruffled edge is level with the top of the cake. Join the ruffle ends tight against each other and smooth out the joining line.

10 For the second ruffle, apply a line of water just below the straight edge of the first ruffle. Repeat these steps for each ruffle, working from the lightest to the darkest shade. The straight edge of the final ruffle should sit flush with the base.

11 Apply the satin ribbon, following the general instructions on page 77, around the bottom edge of the final ruffle.

12 Decide on the position of the peony and carefully insert the wire into the top of the cake.

PRESENT BOX

An oldie but a goody, this is perhaps the most requested cake design at Planet Cake. I had to include it because it's perfect for all celebrations—for engagement parties particularly—and you can change the colours to suit different themes. It looks great in red and white, too: just make sure to read the instructions on using red icing (see page 72) if you want to go there.

MATERIALS

20 cm (8 inch) square cake

syrup

1.02 kg (2 lb 4 oz) ganache

20 cm (8 inch) square cake board

25 cm (10 inch) square cake display board (optional)

1.75 kg (3 lb 13 oz) ready-to-roll pale blue fondant icinge

700 g (1 lb 9 oz) ready-to-roll fondant icing, extra, for display board (optional)

500 g (1 lb 2 oz) ready-to-roll fondant icing, for the bow

cake decorator's alcohol

cornflour (cornstarch), for dusting

EQUIPMENT

ganaching tools

icing tools

rolling pin

pasta machine (optional)

smoothers

paring knife

paintbrush

ruler

modelling tools

piping (icing) bag and #2 piping tip

palette knife

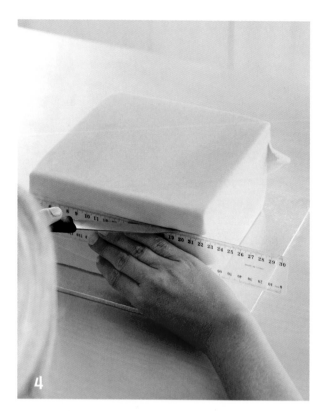

1. Ganache the cake, following the general instructions on how to ganache and prepare square cakes (see page 50). Allow to set overnight.

2. Cover the cake using 1.25 kg (2 lb 12 oz) of the blue fondant icing, following the general instructions on how to cover square cakes (see page 57). Allow to set overnight.

3. If you are using a display board, cover it with the fondant icing, following the general instructions on how to cover cake boards (see page 58). Allow to set overnight.

4. Create a lid for the cake from the remaining blue icing, following the instructions on page 86. Make sure the base layer of fondant is hard before placing the lid.

5. Trim the extra icing from the edges of the lid with a paring knife. Allow to set overnight.

6. Roll the white fondant icing for the bow in a pasta machine or with a rolling pin to approximately 3 mm (⅛ inch) thick. Cut strips 5 cm (2 inches) wide for the ribbons. Brush a small amount of water in a cross on the top of the cake and down the sides where the ribbon will sit. Beginning from the base, stick the ribbon strips to the cake.

7. Use a paring knife to cut the icing to form points at the centre of the cake that all fit together to keep the icing level.

8. Make a bow from white fondant icing, following the general instructions on page 88 and cutting two 5 cm (2 inch) wide ribbons for the tails at the same time. Place the tails on the centre of the ribbon and adhere the bow on top with a dab of water.

SPRINKLES

Sprinkles have been very on-trend and I have included this design because it is just so dead easy, seriously! It is a really fun design, although it's just a bit messy when working with the sprinkles. Remember to use a tray!

MATERIALS

15 cm (6 inch) round cake
20 cm (8 inch) round cake
syrup
1.3 kg (3 lb) ganache
15 cm (6 inch) round cake board
20 cm (8 inch) round cake board
25 cm (10 inch) round cake display board (optional)
1.7 kg (3 lb 12 oz) ready-to-roll white fondant icing
650 g (1 lb 7 oz) ready-to-roll fondant icing, extra, for display board (optional)
cornflour (cornstarch), for dusting
piping gel
500 g (1 lb 2 oz) sprinkles
50 g (1¾ oz) ready-to-roll fondant icing, extra, for heart
10 cm (4 inches) 18-gauge wire
40 g (1½ oz) gold edible glitter
butchers' skewers, for stacking
2 m (79 inches) of 12 mm (½ inch) red satin ribbon

EQUIPMENT

ganaching tools
icing tools
paring knife
pastry brush
medium-size paintbrush
cornflour shaker
scissors
small and large rolling pins
waxed cardboard
5 cm (2 inch) heart cutter
baking tray (or similar)
styrofoam block (optional)
pasta machine (optional)

1 Ganache the cakes, following the instructions on how to ganache and prepare round cakes (see page 48). Allow to set overnight.

2 Cover the cakes with the white fondant icing, following the general instructions on how to cover round cakes (see page 54). Allow to set overnight.

3 If you are using a display board, cover it with the fondant icing, following the general instructions on how to cover cake boards (see page 58). Allow to set overnight.

SPRINKLES

4   Use a pastry brush to cover the side of the base tier of the cake with piping gel. Pour about two-thirds of the sprinkles onto a tray and use your hand to pat the sprinkles onto the side of the cake.

5   Allow the side to dry a little, then brush the top of the tier with piping gel.

6   Pour the remaining sprinkles over the top of the tier. Use your fingers to gently rub the sprinkles onto the top of the tier, letting the tray catch the excess. Once the gel is dry, gently brush any excess sprinkles off and transfer the cake to a display stand or covered display board.

HEART

7 Roll out the extra white fondant icing for the heart to 5 mm (¼ inch) thick: just thick enough to insert the wire. Cut a heart shape with the cutter and insert the wire halfway into the heart from the base point.

8 Brush the heart with piping gel and cover it with gold edible glitter (see page 80 for general instructions about working with edible glitter). Push the wire into a styrofoam block to hold the heart upright while it dries completely.

FINISHING

9 Stack the plain cake on top of the tier with sprinkles, following the general instructions for stacking cakes on page 60.

10 Trim both tiers with satin ribbon, following the general instructions on page 77.

11 Use a ruler to find the centre of the cake and poke the wired heart into the top tier of the cake.

WEDDING CAKES

This is definitely the most important type of cake, because couples will remember their wedding cake and the person who made it for years to come. At Planet Cake, I often have couples approach me gushing with delight about a wedding cake we made for them ten years earlier. So just imgaine how fondly your friends or loved ones would remember your efforts if you were to take it upon yourself to bake their wedding cake. Take ample time to prepare and make sure that your cake design will feed the required number of people and suit the wedding theme and the couple. Please do not feel that you have to make a professional wedding cake to exacting standards. Only you will be able to see any fault in the cake; cake decorators are almost always critical of their own work. The success of a wedding cake always lies in the flavour and the design rather than it being one hundred per cent perfect: on this piece of advice you are just going to have to trust me!

JEWELLED FLOWERS

This cake design is perfect for the modern romantic: the square cakes are a modern shape that has been softened with the delicate flowers.

MATERIALS

15 cm (6 inch) square cake
20 cm (8 inch) square cake
syrup
1.7 kg (3 lb 12 oz) ganache
15 cm (6 inch) square cake board
20 cm (8 inch) square cake board
25 cm (10 inch) square cake display
  board (optional)
2.1 kg (4 lb 10 oz) ready-to-roll
  ivory fondant icing
700 g (1 lb 7 oz) ready-to-roll
  fondant icing, extra, for display
  board (optional)
cornflour (cornstarch), for dusting
butchers' skewers (for stacking)
2 m (79 inches) of 15 mm ($\frac{5}{8}$ inch)
  cream satin ribbon
2 m (79 inches) of 10 mm ($\frac{3}{8}$ inch)
  pale pink satin ribbon
double-sided adhesive tape
royal icing
250 g (9 oz) flower paste
  (see page 43)
sugar glue
sugar pearls
edible crystals (or flat-backed
  diamantés)
tiny cachous

EQUIPMENT

ganaching tools
icing tools
small rolling pin
rose petal cutters
ball tool and petal pad
frilling tool
apple tray
piping (icing) bag and #2 piping tip
tweezers
paring knife
paintbrush
pins
scissors

1 Ganache the cakes, following the general instructions on how to ganache and prepare square cakes (see page 50). Allow to set overnight.

2 Cover the cakes with the ivory fondant icing, following the general instructions on how to cover square cakes (see page 57). Allow to set overnight.

3 If you are using a display board, cover it with the extra fondant icing, following the general instructions on how to cover cake boards (see page 58). Allow to set overnight.

4 Stack the cakes, following the general instructions on page 60. Carefully transfer the cakes to the display stand or covered cake display board.

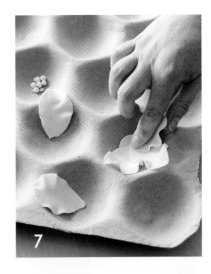

5 Apply the wider cream ribbon to the base of each tier, following the general instructions on page 77. Apply the pale pink ribbon over the top, following the same method.

6 Roll out the flower paste to 2 mm (1/32 inch) thick and use the rose petal cutters to cut five petals for each flower (40 petals for eight flowers). Thin the edge of each petal using a ball tool on a petal pad and add a slight ruffle to the thinned edges with the frilling tool.

7 Place the petals in the hollows of an apple tray and use sugar glue to stick the points of the petals together in the centre, creating a flower.

8 Put sugar glue in the flower centre and place pearls, crystals and cachous in the glue using tweezers.

9 Leave the flowers in the apple tray until they are almost dry. It's best to place them on the cake while they are still slightly soft so that any gaps can be filled and petals interlocked.

10 Fill a piping (icing) bag with royal icing and use it to adhere the flowers to the cake in a cascade down the front side. Be careful as the flowers are fragile.

THE LOVE BOAT

This is one of my favourite cakes because I had a nautical theme for my own wedding. The design is timeless and this can be a great cake for an event at a marina, on a boat or a beach. You can see the effect of combining different-shape cakes (a square and a round) and I have also introduced horizontal stripes.

You can create an entirely different cake by changing the motif and the colours; for example, white and yellow with a simple duck would be great for a baby's cake.

MATERIALS

peony flower (see page 112)

15 cm (6 inch) square cake

20 cm (8 inch) round cake

syrup

1.45 kg (3 lb 3 oz) ganache

15 cm (6 inch) square cake board

20 cm (8 inch) round cake board

three 25 cm (10 inch) round cake display boards

1.8 kg (4 lb) ready-to-roll white fondant icing

650 g (1 lb 7 oz) ready-to-roll white fondant icing, extra, for display board

500 g (1 lb 2 oz) ready-to-roll fondant icing, for decorations

royal blue food colouring paste

cornflour (cornstarch), for dusting

piping gel

85 cm (33½ inches) of 2 cm (¾ inch) wide red and white striped ribbon

1.2 m (47 inches) of 4 mm (⅛ inch) white cord

butchers' skewers, for stacking

anchor motif printout

Tylose powder

sugar glue

EQUIPMENT

ganaching tools

icing tools

craft bond adhesive

paring knife

small and large rolling pins

frilling tool

2B pencil

tape measure

pizza cutter

cardboard

scissors

vinyl sheet

small and medium paintbrushes

1. Make the peony, following the instructions on page 112. Allow drying time of at least 24 hours, preferably more.

2. Ganache the cakes, following the general instructions on how to ganache and prepare round and square cakes (see pages 48 and 50). Allow to set overnight.

3. Cover the cakes with the fondant icing, following the general instructions on how to cover round and square cakes (see pages 54 and 57). Allow to set overnight.

4. For an extra-thick round display board, glue three boards together in a stack using craft bond adhesive (the edges will be covered with ribbon). Cover the top board with the fondant icing, following the general instructions on how to cover display boards (see page 58). Allow to set overnight.

HORIZONTAL STRIPES

5. Divide the icing for the decorations into four parts and set one quarter aside to remain white. Colour the remaining icing royal blue. It's a good idea to colour the icing the day before decorating the cake, as it will make your job a lot more challenging if the icing is still soft.

6. Use a tape measure to measure the height and circumference of the bottom tier. Divide the height by 3 to determine the width of the stripes. Create an icing guide by cutting a cardboard strip to the right dimensions, making sure that the length is at least 5 cm (2 inches) inches longer than the circumference measurement.

7. Roll out the blue and the white icing thinly using a large rolling pin and use the cardboard strip as a guide to cut two blue stripes and one white stripe, using a pizza cutter. Place the stripes underneath a vinyl sheet so they don't dry out.

8. Starting with the bottom stripe, use a paintbrush to apply a little water or piping gel around the base of the cake.

9. Roll a blue stripe onto a small rolling pin and carefully unroll it in position on the cake. Make sure the join is at the back and use a sharp knife to cut the overlap so the ends of the stripe are flush.

10. Repeat the process with the white stripe and then the second blue stripe, ensuring that the edges of the stripes are flush and the top of the blue stripe is level with the top of the cake. Trim off any excess icing with a paring knife.

11 Carefully transfer the striped cake to the display board. Trim the edges of the stacked display boards with the red and white striped ribbon, following the instructions on page 77. When finished, tie the white cord around the middle of the ribbon, knotting the ends in the front. Trim the ends of the cord.

12 Stack the square cake on top of the round cake, following the general instructions for stacking two-tier cakes on page 60.

13 Make the blue braid trim by rolling two thin sausages of blue icing (following the instructions on page 84) to at least 60 cm (24 inches) in length. Twist the two strands together to make a rope and place it carefully around the base of the square cake, joining the ends at the back of the cake by cutting them flush and adhering them with a dab of water.

14 To create the anchor motif (or any motif of your choice), print it out at the desired size from your computer or draw it freehand and cut it out of cardboard to make a template. Roll the remaining royal blue icing out thinly and use the template to cut out the shape. Allow the shape to dry out a little under a vinyl sheet. Adhere to the centre front of the square cake using a dab of water.

15 Place the peony on top of the cake.

The horizontal stripes can be a little daunting, but they are easy enough to make. If you are cautious, stay away from dark icing colours such as red and black, because dark icing is softer and can be more challenging to use.

DAMASK CAKE

One of the most popular cake-decorating techniques is stencilling; it saves hours of piping time and allows you to cover large surface areas. The thing about this technique is that your cake will completely change depending on which stencil you choose, and there are literally thousands to choose from. I have also included instructions on how to create your own stencil, as you may want to replicate a pattern from the invitation or a monogram.

MATERIALS

two peony flowers (see page 112)
15 cm (6 inch) square cake
20 cm (8 inch) square cake
25 cm (10 inch) square cake
syrup
3.2 kg (7 lb 1 oz) ganache
15 cm (6 inch) square cake board
20 cm (8 inch) square cake board
25 cm (10 inch) square cake board
35 cm (14 inch) square cake display board (optional)
4 kg (9 lb) ready-to-roll ivory fondant icing
1 kg (2 lb 4 oz) ready-to-roll fondant icing, extra, for display board (optional)
royal icing
lustre dust (optional)
cornflour (cornstarch), for dusting
butchers' skewers, for stacking
3 m (120 inches) of 12 mm (½ inch) wide white satin ribbon

EQUIPMENT

ganaching tools
icing tools
rolling pin
cake smoothers
flexiscraper
paring knife
paintbrush
pastry brush
palette knife
pins
turntable
ruler
scissors
stencil (see page 80)
scraper
metal ruler
masking tape

1 Make the petals, centre and leaves for the peonies, following the instructions on page 112. Allow to dry for at least 24 hours.

2 Ganache the cakes, following the general instructions on how to ganache and prepare square cakes (see page 50). Allow to set overnight.

3 Cover the cakes with the ivory fondant icing, following the general instructions on how to cover square cakes (see page 57). Allow to set overnight.

4 If you are using a display board, cover it with the fondant icing, following the general instructions on how to cover display boards (see page 58). Allow to set overnight.

STENCILLING

5 Follow the general instructions on page 80 to make a stencil, or use a ready-made stencil from a cake-decorating supplier.

6 Make the royal icing. Carefully tape the stencil to the cake using masking tape, which is easy to peel away when you have finished.

7 Use a palette knife to spread the royal icing liberally over the stencil. Take care not to go over the edge of the tape.

8 Using a metal scraper, gently but firmly scrape the excess royal icing away from the stencil.

9 Carefully peel the stencil and tape away, taking care not to smudge the royal icing.

10 Make sure one side is dry before stencilling another and repeat for all sides of each tier.

11 Gently brush lustre dust over the dried royal icing, if you wish.

FINISHING

12 Stack the cakes, following the general instructions for stacking tiered cakes on page 60. Carefully transfer the cakes to the display stand or covered display board.

13 Following the general instructions on page 77, place satin ribbon around the base of each tier.

14 Assemble the peonies, following the instructions on page 112. Place the peonies in position on the cake.

The peonies can be made weeks in advance of the cake. Keep them dry and in a cool place. This is a good way to manage your decorating time.

If the icing is smearing as you stencil, tape a layer of tulle (available from haberdashery stores) over the top of the stencil and apply the royal icing through the tulle.

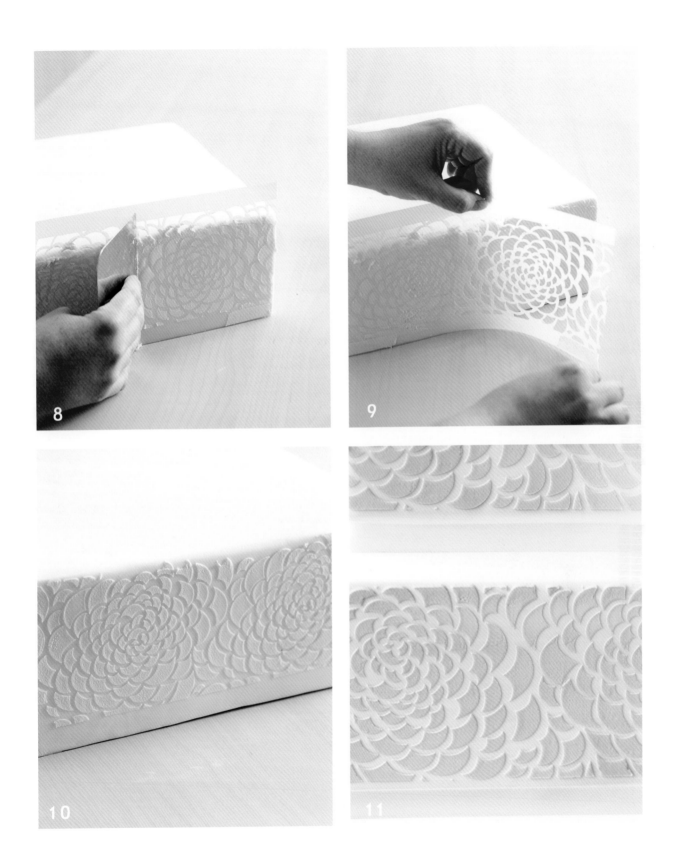

DIAMANTÉS

This cake, with individually placed diamantés, is a bit time-consuming, but it is worth the effort if you have the time. If you are short of time, the Pink Bling cake on page 172 offers a fast alternative using ready-made ropes of diamantés. You can apply the diamantés to one or all sides of the cake, depending on how much time you have; it looks great with sugar flowers or fresh flowers as well, or keep it sleek and simple. Under a spotlight and on a mirrored surface it is truly spectacular. Make sure to advise the kitchen to remove the diamantés with a paring knife before cutting.

MATERIALS

15 cm (6 inch) square cake
20 cm (8 inch) square cake
25 cm (10 inch) square cake
syrup
3.2 kg (7 lb 1 oz) ganache
15 cm (6 inch) square cake board
20 cm (8 inch) square cake board
25 cm (10 inch) square cake board
35 cm (14 inch) square cake display
    board (optional)
4 kg (9 lb) ready-to-roll white
    fondant icing
1 kg (2 lb 4 oz) ready-to-roll
    fondant icing, extra, for display
    board (optional)
cornflour (cornstarch), for dusting
butchers' skewers, for stacking
1500 flat-back diamanté crystals
piping gel
2.5 m (98½ inches) of 10 mm
    (⅜ inch) wide black satin ribbon

EQUIPMENT

ganaching tools
icing tools
pastry brush
fine paintbrush
ruler
vinyl sheet
pizza cutter
baking paper
2B pencil
scissors
tape measure
tweezers, to apply diamantés
pins
modelling tools

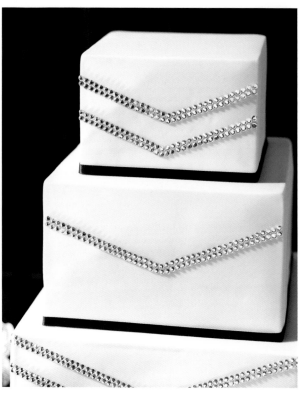

1 Ganache the cakes, following the general instructions on how to ganache and prepare square cakes (see page 50). Allow to set overnight.

2 Cover the cakes with the white fondant icing, following the general instructions on how to cover square cakes (see page 57). Allow to set overnight.

3 If you are using a display board, cover it with the extra fondant icing, following the general instructions on how to cover display boards (see page 58). Allow to set overnight.

4 Stack the cakes, following the general instructions on page 60. Carefully transfer the cakes to the display stand or covered cake display board.

5 To create a template for the crystals, cut baking paper to the same dimensions as the side of the bottom tier. Fold the rectangle in half vertically, make a centre crease and then open it out again. Use a ruler and pencil to draw a line diagonally from one corner to the other in both directions. The V shape formed by the top halves of these lines is the basic line for diamantés. Rule another V shape 3 cm (1¼ inches) below the first one for the second line of diamantés, for the top and bottom tiers.

6 Use the pin prick method or the tracing method (see page 78) to transfer the lines to the sides of the cake. You can decorate only the front face of each tier, or place diamantés on all four sides. Move the base line down the side of the cake for the middle and top tiers.

7 Use a fine paintbrush to apply a thin line of piping gel along the lines.

8 Use tweezers to place each diamante, offsetting the two rows of diamantés from each other so they fit together nicely. Alternatively, place a tiny ball of icing on the end of a modelling tool and use it to pick up and place the individual diamantés.

9 Apply the black satin ribbon around the base of each tier, following the general instructions on page 77.

PINK BLING

I have some clients who just cannot get enough bling. This look is really easy to achieve and looks great in other colours as well. You can buy the strings of diamantés from haberdashery or cake-decorating suppliers; if you want more sparkle you can double or even triple the amount of rope you use. At night, under the lights, this cake just pops and if you display it on a mirror it looks wonderful. Just make sure to advise the kitchen to remove the rope before cutting.

MATERIALS

15 cm (6 inch) round cake

20 cm (8 inch) round cake

25 cm (10 inch) round cake

syrup

2.5 kg (5 lb 8 oz) ganache

15 cm (6 inch) round cake board

20 cm (8 inch) round cake board

25 cm (10 inch) round cake board

35 cm (14 inch) round cake display board (optional)

3.2 kg (7 lb 1 oz) ready-to-roll pink fondant icing

900 g (2 lb) ready-to-roll fondant icing, extra, for display board (optional)

cornflour (cornstarch), for dusting

butchers' skewers, for stacking

500 g (1 lb 2 oz) ready-to-roll pink fondant icing, extra (for the bow)

3 m (120 inches) diamanté rope

royal icing

EQUIPMENT

ganaching tools

icing tools

pasta machine (optional)

paring knife

pizza cutter

pastry brush

vinyl sheet

scissors

medium-size paintbrush

cornflour shaker

tape measure

scissors

ruler

piping (icing) bag and #2 piping tip

1   Ganache the cakes, following the general instructions on how to ganache and prepare round cakes (see page 48). Allow to set overnight.

2   To create the pretty pink hue we have used for our icing you will use red food colouring paste with a touch of brown colouring paste and an even smaller amount of black. Cover the cakes with the pink fondant icing, following the general instructions on how to cover round cakes (see page 54). Allow to set overnight.

3   If you are using a display board, cover it with the fondant icing, following the general instructions on how to cover display boards (see page 58). Allow to set overnight.

4   Stack the cakes, following the general instructions for stacking tiered cakes on page 60. Carefully transfer the cakes to a display stand or covered display board.

BOW AND DIAMANTÉS

5   Using the pink coloured icing for the bow, sprinkle a small amount of cornflour on the work surface and roll out the icing with a small rolling pin, to approximately 1.5 mm (1/32 inch) thick. Alternatively, use a pasta machine.

6   Make a bow, following the general instructions on page 88, and cut strips approximately 4 cm (1½ inches) wide for the ribbon tails and the smaller bow loops in front of the main loops.

7   Place the ribbon tails on the top tier and then place the bow loops on top. Wrap a small section of icing around the join between the bow loops.

8   Measure the circumference of each tier with a tape measure to determine the length of diamante string you need. Wrap the diamantés around the base of each tier and cut it to length. Pipe royal icing to secure the ends of the string, holding them in place for a few seconds until they are firmly adhered.

9   Use short pieces of diamanté string to decorate the centre of the bow, adhering the diamantés in place with royal icing.

PASTEL CHINA RIBBONS

This cake is a great design, because the colour of the icing ribbons can be changed to match any theme. You really cannot go wrong. The gold trim sets it off and is easy to achieve; however, it is not essential. Any colour can be used.

MATERIALS

15 cm (6 inch) round cake

20 cm (8 inch) round cake

25 cm (10 inch) round cake

syrup

2.5 kg (5 lb 8 oz) ganache

rose (see page 106)

peony leaves (see page 115), painted with edible gold paint

5 cm (6 inch) round cake board

20 cm (8 inch) round cake board

25 cm (10 inch) round cake board

30 cm (12 inch) round cake display board (optional)

3.2 kg (6 lb 13 oz) ready-to-roll white fondant icing

850 g (1 lb 14 oz) ready-to-roll fondant icing, extra, for display board (optional)

800 g (1 lb 12 oz) ready-to-roll fondant icing, extra, for ribbons

red, blue, green, brown and black food colouring paste

cornflour (cornstarch), for dusting

royal icing

edible gold lustre dust

cake decorator's alcohol

EQUIPMENT

ganaching tools

icing tools

pasta machine (optional)

paring knife

tape measure

ruler

pizza cutter

vinyl sheet

fine and medium paintbrushes

cornflour shaker

flexiscraper

piping (icing) bag and #1 or #2 piping tip

1 Ganache the cakes, following the general instructions on how to ganache and prepare round cakes (see page 48). Allow to set overnight.

2 Make the petals, centre and leaves for the rose, following the instructions on page 106. Note that we have used peony leaves (page 115) painted gold, rather than rose leaves. Allow to dry for at least 24 hours.

3 Cover the cakes with the white fondant icing, following the general instructions on how to cover round cakes (see page 54). Allow to set overnight.

4 If you are using a display board, cover it with the extra fondant icing, following the general instructions on how to cover display boards (see page 58). Allow to set overnight.

5 Stack the cakes, following the general instructions on page 60. Carefully transfer the cakes to the display stand or covered board.

6 Divide the fondant icing for the ribbons into three portions and colour each part with food colouring paste. To achieve the pastel tints, use a small amount of paste and follow the general instructions on page 72 to ensure even coverage. You may need to add very small amounts of brown or black colour to the blue, green and red to create the desired tones.

7 Roll out each colour of icing to 2 mm (1/16 inch) thick. Cut strips 4 cm (1½ inches) wide.

Measure the circumference of each tier of the cake and use a ruler and pizza cutter to cut the strips to this length plus 5 cm (2 inches). Keep the strips covered with a vinyl sheet when you are not working with them to prevent them drying out.

8 Lightly brush a line of water around the base of the tier on which you wish to place the strip. Roll the strip onto a small rolling pin and carefully unroll it around the cake.

9 Overlap the ends of the strip and cut them with a sharp knife so that they meet perfectly. Make sure the join is at the back of the cake. Repeat with the remaining tiers and coloured icing strips.

10 Fill a piping (icing) bag with royal icing and, using a #2 nozzle, pipe a line of small dots at even intervals along the top edge of the fondant ribbon. You can use a pin to mark even spacing for the dots before you start, if you wish. Begin at the top tier and work your way down to avoid bumping fresh piping.

11 Once the rose leaves and the piping dots are dry, gently paint them with a mixture of gold lustre dust and cake decorator's alcohol using a fine paintbrush. Allow to dry completely.

12 Assemble the rose with the gold leaves and place it on the cake, following the instructions on page 106.

VINTAGE RUFFLES

This is a cake that our students have tackled in the Planet Cake school, with amazing results. You can play around with the design: you may want to quilt all of the tiers of the cake or have every tier ruffled. It is more time-consuming than the other cakes that I have included in this book and you will need to dedicate at least two days to the decorating alone, as the ruffles and quilting take a lot of time and effort; however, the effect is worth it. Super pretty!

MATERIALS

peony flower (see page 112)
15 cm (6 inch) round cake
20 cm (8 inch) round cake
25 cm (10 inch) round cake
syrup
2.5 kg (5 lb 8 oz) chocolate ganache
15 cm (6 inch) round cake board
20 cm (8 inch) round cake board
25 cm (10 inch) round cake board
30 cm (12 inch) round cake display board (optional)
3.5 kg (7 lb 14 oz) ready-to-roll white fondant icing
850 g (1 lb 14 oz) ready-to-roll fondant icing, extra, for display board (optional)
cornflour (cornstarch), for dusting
royal icing
butchers' skewers, for stacking
2 m (79 inches) of 10 mm (⅜ inch) pale pink satin ribbon

EQUIPMENT

ganaching tools
icing tools
tape measure
pins
ruler
set square
piping (icing) bag and #2 piping tip
paring knife
pizza cutter
vinyl sheet
medium paintbrush
cornflour shaker
pasta machine (optional)
frilling tool
scissors
turntable

1 Make the petals, centre and leaves for the peony, following the instructions on page 112. Allow to dry for at least 24 hours.

2 Ganache the cakes, following the general instructions on how to ganache and prepare round cakes (see page 48). Allow to set overnight.

3 Cover the bottom and top tier cakes with the white fondant icing, following the general instructions on how to cover round cakes (see page 54). Allow to set overnight.

4 If you are using a display board, cover it with the extra fondant icing, following the general instructions on how to cover display boards (see page 58). Allow to set overnight.

QUILTING

5 The middle tier needs to be quilted as soon as it is covered. Cover the cake, following the general instructions on page 54, then measure the circumference and height. Place the tier on a turntable, to make your work easier, if you wish.

6 Use a tape measure and a pin to mark every 2.5 cm (1 inch) around the base of the tier.

7 Hold the set square with one side flush with the bottom edge of the cake and gently roll the diagonal edge against the cake to create an indent.

8 Once the lines have been marked in one direction all around the cake, follow the same steps in the opposite direction to create diamond shapes.

9 Finally, use the point of a frilling tool to indent the icing where the lines cross. After the cake is assembled you'll pipe dots of royal icing into the indents.

FINISHING

10 Stack the cakes, following the general instructions on page 60. Carefully transfer them to the display stand or covered board.

11 Following the general instructions on piping with royal icing (see page 82), pipe a fine line around the base of the quilted tier to cover the join. You could also use narrow white ribbon, following the instructions on page 77.

12 Pipe royal icing into the indents on the quilted cake. These can be coloured if you wish.

13 Make ruffles for the bottom tier of the cake from the remaining fondant icing, following the general instructions on page 85. For this cake, the ruffles begin at the bottom of the cake and the top strip has both edges ruffled with the frilling tool.

14 Wrap a length of satin ribbon around the centre of the top ruffle, following the general instructions on placing ribbon on page 77.

15 Wrap a length of satin ribbon around the top tier following the general instructions on placing ribbon on page 77.

16 Assemble the peony, following the instructions on page 112, and place it on the top of the finished cake.

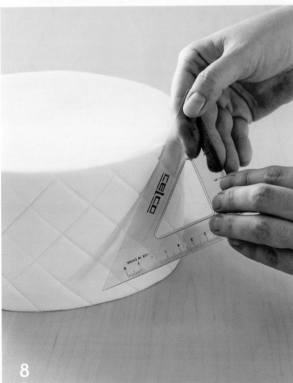

WELCOMING BABY

When my daughter was born, I was so excited I actually had two events: one was a naming day in Sydney and then the official christening was held in England. I was so adamant that everything be perfect, I had her christening cake flown to Heathrow airport from Australia. I think I might have gone a little over the top! Whether the event is a christening, naming day, baptism, baby shower or child's birthday, all of these cake designs will be a success. You can alter the colours to suit, interchange the decorations and even get creative and use some other techniques in this book to design your own; for example, a single-tier cake with a beautiful sugar peony would be delightful.

TWO CATS

This is a very cute little cake: I have done so many cakes for cat-lovers that I thought I would include it as a cute option for celebrating twins. The bunting is simple to create and can be used for many cake designs. Transform the mood of this cake with brighter colours or by changing the expression on the cats' faces.

MATERIALS

two cat figurines (use the basic
    instructions on page 96)
20 cm (8 inch) round cake
syrup
800 g (1 lb 12 oz) ganache
20 cm (8 inch) round cake board
25 cm (10 inch) round cake display
    board (optional)
1 kg (2 lb 4 oz) ready-to-roll
    fondant icing
650 g (1 lb 7 oz) ready-to-roll
    fondant icing, extra, for display
    board (optional)
cornflour (cornstarch)
70 cm (27½ inches) of 2 cm
    (¾ inch) wide taupe satin ribbon
sugar glue
skewers and drinking straws,
    for flagpoles
40 cm (16 inches) of kitchen string
small pieces of 12 mm (½ inch)
    wide patterned ribbons,
    in several patterns
double-sided adhesive tape
30 cm (12 inches) of 6 mm (¼ inch)
    wide satin ribbons, each of three
    different colours
2 small balls coloured fondant icing

EQUIPMENT

ganaching tools
icing tools
paring knife
small rolling pin
frilling tool
toothpicks
small and medium paintbrushes
modelling tools
small scissors

1. Make the cat figurines, following the instructions for animal figurines on page 96.

2. Add a contrasting belly to the body; pinch the ears into triangles; and use the frilling tool to make small holes for whiskers on the face. Add a bow if the cat is to represent a girl. Add a sausage of coloured icing for a tail. Allow drying time of at least 24 hours, preferably more.

3. Ganache the cake, following the general instructions on how to ganache and prepare round cakes (see page 48). Allow to set overnight.

4. Cover the cake with the fondant icing, following the general instructions on how to cover round cakes (see page 54). Allow to set overnight.

5. Cover the display board, if using, with the fondant icing, following the general instructions on how to cover display boards (see page 58). Allow to set overnight.

6. Carefully transfer the cake to the display board or cake stand. Trim the base of the cake with the 2 cm (¾ inch) wide satin ribbon, following the instructions on page 77.

7. Place the figurines on top of the cake and adhere them with sugar glue or a dab of water.

BUNTING

8. Make poles for the bunting by inserting a kitchen skewer inside a decorative drinking straw.

9. Tie kitchen string between the poles, allowing 22 cm (8½ inches) between the poles. Fold short lengths of the patterned ribbon over the string and stick them together with double-sided adhesive tape, then cut an inverted V-shape out of the bottom of each flag with scissors.

10. Cut the narrow satin ribbons in half and secure them to the top of each pole. Roll two small balls of coloured fondant icing and place one at the top of each pole for decoration.

11. Carefully lift the poles and bunting onto the top of the cake and push the skewers in at an angle to hold the arrangement in place. Trim the hanging ribbons and string to a suitable length.

WHAT A HOOT

If you are a complete beginner or just want a relatively quick result then this design is absolutely perfect. You could make it even easier with a round cake instead of a square. Owls and bunting are perfect for a boy or a girl, a christening or a birthday. I have made the round bunting to imitate lanterns; however, if you would like to make them traditional flags then just cut triangles instead of circles. Have fun!

MATERIALS

owlet figurine (see page 100)
18 cm (7 inch) square cake
syrup
850 g (1 lb 14 oz) ganache
18 cm (7 inch) square cake board
three 22 cm (9 inch) square cake
    display boards
1 kg (2 lb 4 oz) ready-to-roll
    fondant icing
650 g (1 lb 7 oz) ready-to-roll
    fondant icing, extra, for display
    board
160 g (5¾ oz) ready-to-roll fondant
    icing, extra, for mat and bunting
food colouring paste, various
    colours
cornflour (cornstarch)
75 cm (29 inches) of 12 mm
    (½ inch) wide white satin ribbon
90 cm (35½ inches) of 10 mm
    (⅜ inch) wide pale pink or blue
    satin ribbon
90 cm (35½ inches) of 15 mm
    (⅝ inch) wide darker pink or blue
    grosgrain ribbon

EQUIPMENT

ganaching tools
icing tools
barbecue skewer
craft bond adhesive
paring knife
small rolling pin
#2 piping (icing) tip
dinner plate (template)
toothpick
crinkle cutter
circle cutter set
small and medium paintbrushes
modelling tools

1   Make the owl figurine, following the instructions on page 100. Allow drying time of at least 24 hours, preferably more. For added support, insert a barbecue skewer into the base of the owlet before it dries.

2   Ganache the cake, following the general instructions on how to ganache and prepare square cakes (see page 50). Allow to set overnight.

3   Cover the cake with the fondant icing, following the general instructions on how to cover square cakes (see page 57). Allow to set overnight.

4   For an extra thick square display board, glue three boards together in a stack using craft bond adhesive (the edges will be covered with ribbon). Cover the top board with the fondant icing, following the general instructions on how to cover cake boards (see page 58). Allow to set overnight.

5   Carefully transfer the cake to the covered display board.

FIGURINE

6   Roll out a small amount of coloured icing for the mat. Using a large circle cutter or a crinkle cutter, cut out a disc of icing. Use a #2 piping tip to make small round impressions around the edge of the mat. Adhere the mat to the centre of the cake with a dab of water.

7   Shorten the skewer in the owl figurine if necessary and insert it into the centre of the cake through the mat. Use a dab of water or sugar glue to fix the figurine to the icing.

LANTERN BUNTING

8   To get a perfect arc, rest a dinner plate against the side of the cake with the edges aligned with the corners, and use a toothpick to gently prick along the curved edge.

9   Roll a very thin strand of fondant, following the instructions on page 84, to lay along the marked arc. Adhere it to the icing with a dab of water.

10 To make the lantern circles, colour small amounts of fondant icing with various colours and roll them out thinly using the small rolling pin. Use a small circle cutter (15 mm/⅝ inch) to cut the circle shapes. Gently roll with the small rolling pin to smooth them if necessary, being careful not to put too much pressure.

11 Adhere the circles to the cake just below the fondant arc, using a medium paintbrush to apply small dabs of water.

FINISHING

12 Trim the base of the cake with the 12 mm (½ inch) wide white satin ribbon, following the instructions on page 77. Trim the edges of the stacked display boards with the pink (or blue) satin and grosgrain ribbons, following the same instructions.

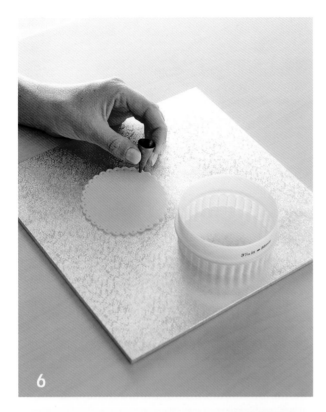

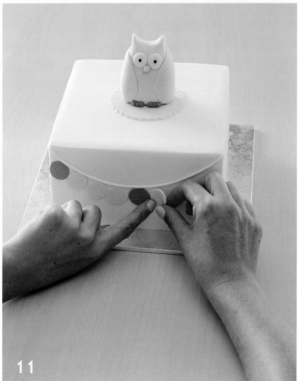

TEDDY BEAR CAKE

One of the most popular designs ever, perfect for boys and girls and all children's events, the only essential element is a very cute teddy figurine. The bear can be made well in advance if you want to save time. The cake base looks great in all shades of gelato colours and you can personalise it as much as you wish using alphabet cutters. You may want to leave the blossoms off and just put the child's name in cut-outs on the side: this always looks great.

MATERIALS

15 cm (6 inch) square cake

syrup

700 g (1 lb 9 oz) ganache

teddy bear figurine (see page 96)

15 cm (6 inch) square cake board

20 cm (8 inch) square cake display board (optional)

1 kg (2 lb 4 oz) ready-to-roll fondant icing

550 g (1 lb 4 oz) ready-to-roll fondant icing, extra, for display board (optional)

food colouring paste

cornflour (cornstarch), for dusting

1 m (39½ inches) of 10 mm (⅜ inch) wide white satin ribbon (or colour to match icing)

EQUIPMENT

ganaching tools

icing tools

vinyl sheet

pastry brush

piping (icing) bag and #2 piping tip

paring knife

medium paintbrush

pasta machine (optional)

small flower, leaf and alphabet cutters

flower plunger cutter

frilling tool and petal pad

large circle cutter

1   Ganache the cake, following the general instructions on how to ganache and prepare square cakes (see page 50). Allow to set overnight.

2   Make the teddy bear, following the instructions on page 96. Allow to dry for at least 24 hours.

3   Cover the cake with the fondant icing, following the general instructions on how to cover square cakes (see page 57). Allow to set overnight.

4   If you are using a display board, cover it with the extra fondant icing, following the general instructions on how to cover display boards (see page 58). Allow to set overnight.

GARLAND OF FLOWERS

5   Roll out small amounts of coloured fondant icing to about 2 mm (1/16 inch) thick. Keep the pieces you are not using under a vinyl sheet to prevent them drying out.

6   Use a small petal cutter to cut leaves from pale green icing.

7   Pinch the end of each leaf to give it a little curl.

8   Use a flower plunger cutter to cut daisies from purple and white icing. Cut smaller flowers from white icing. Cut an initial letter if you want to use one.

9   Use a frilling tool to shape and curl the daisy petals slightly. Follow the instructions on page 127 to make several small rolled roses in pink and white icing.

10 Press a large round cutter into the fondant to mark a circle on the front of the cake.

11 Arrange the blossoms and leaves around the circle, adhering them with a tiny dab of water. Place the initial letter in the centre following the general instructions on page 76.

FINISHING

12 Carefully transfer the cake to a display stand or covered display board.

13 Roll out a small amount of icing for the mat. Using a large circle cutter or a crinkle cutter, cut out a disc of icing. Use a #2 piping tip to make small round impressions all over the mat for a lacy look. Adhere the mat to the centre of the cake with a dab of water.

14 Place the teddy bear figurine in the centre of the mat.

15 Trim the base of the cake with white satin ribbon, following the general instructions on page 77.

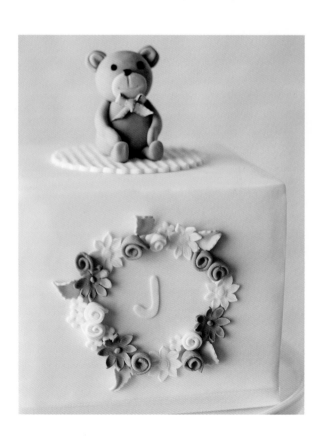

BABY BIRD

I have styled this cake with the idea of creating a little woodland, inspired by so many events I have attended recently in which wood and other natural products were used to create a gorgeous rustic feel. The baby bird figurine is very simple and would be perfect as a decoration for many other cakes. The additional woodland decorations are easy to create using your fingers and a few shape cutters. Baby Bird is a really fun and whimsical cake and the figurines are so enjoyable to create: older children would love to help, so why not share the process and spend time together?

MATERIALS

baby bird and nest figurine (see page 102)
200 g (7 oz) ready-to-roll fondant icing, extra, for decorations
food colouring paste
Tylose powder
paint, for details
petal dust
sugar glue
18 cm (7 inch) round cake
syrup
650 g (1 lb 7 oz) ganache
18 cm (7 inch) round cake board
23 cm (9 inch) round cake display board
23 cm (9 inch) round cake tin lid, approximately 3 cm (1¼ inches) deep
1 kg (2 lb 4 oz) ready-to-roll fondant icing
600 g (1 lb 5 oz) ready-to-roll fondant icing, extra, for display board
cornflour (cornstarch)
75 cm (29½ inches) of 12 mm (½ inch) wide brown satin ribbon
75 cm (29½ inches) of 2 cm (¾ inch) wide ecru twill ribbon
75 cm (29½ inches) of 6 mm (¼ inch) wide gold velvet ribbon

EQUIPMENT

ganaching tools
icing tools
paring knife
pizza cutter
masking tape
small rolling pin
toothpicks
leaf cutters
small and medium paintbrushes
modelling tools

FIGURINE AND DECORATIONS

1   Make the baby bird and nest figurine, following the instructions on page 102. Allow drying time of at least 24 hours, preferably more.

2   Colour the icing for the woodland elements as desired. You will need 8 g (¼ oz) of icing for each large mushroom; 6 g (³⁄₁₆ oz) of icing for each acorn; 2 g (¹⁄₁₆ oz) of icing per leaf and 5 g (³⁄₁₆ oz) of icing for the berries. Place the coloured icing in a resealable plastic bag until you are ready to use it, so it doesn't dry out.

3   Roll each icing ball in Tylose powder and knead it in until well combined. Return each ball to the resealable bag before working on the next one.

4   To make the flat mushroom tops, roll balls of icing, use the ball tool to hollow out the underside and smooth the top with your fingers. Score the underside lightly with the back of a paring knife to create the gills. Allow to dry: to add a slight curl, rest them up against something during the drying process.

5   To make the conical mushroom tops, roll a fat little oval shape and squash lightly at one end until it is slightly pointed. Allow to dry.

6   Roll icing rolls for the stalks (see page 84), making sure they are not too long or thin, the longer they are the more difficult it will be to stand them upright. Adhere the stalks to the underside of the mushroom tops using sugar glue or water. Allow to dry, supported with tissues or cotton wool.

7   Roll small balls of icing for the berries. Create a small indentation on one side with a frilling tool. Allow to dry.

If the acorns and mushrooms are too large they will dominate the cake, so keep them small and delicate.

8 To make leaves, roll out a very thin piece of icing, then cut out leaf shapes using a leaf cutter or a paring knife. Score down the centre with the back of the knife or use a leaf veiner to add veins. Use a frilling tool to thin and curl the edges if you wish. Allow to dry, adding a slight twist for a natural look.

9 To make acorns, roll a fat oval shape. Roll out a very thin piece of darker brown icing and use a circle cutter to cut a small round disc. Place the disc on one end of the oval, smooth it down with your fingers to make a little cap and trim off any excess. Use a toothpick to add texture to the cap. Make a tiny icing roll for the stalk, then use a frilling tool to create a little indentation at the top of the acorn; insert the stalk with a dab of water.

10 Once all of your woodland pieces are dry, paint on any details and then lightly dust them with petal dust, a little bit at a time.

DECORATE THE CAKE

11 Ganache the cake, following the general instructions on how to ganache and prepare round cakes (see page 48). Allow to set overnight.

12 Cover the cake with the fondant icing, following the general instructions on how to cover round cakes (see page 54). Allow to set overnight.

13 Cover the display board with the fondant icing, following the general instructions on how to cover display boards (see page 58). Allow to set overnight.

14 Place the display board on top of the cake tin lid and use masking tape to secure them together. Apply ribbons around the top and bottom edges of the cake tin lid, following the general instructions on page 77. Carefully transfer the cake to the board.

15 Place the decorations on the cake and display board. Place the baby bird first, followed by the larger mushrooms and acorns, then the leaves and berries. Arrange the decorations first—to make sure you are happy with the placement and that there are no gaps—before you stick them down with sugar glue.

ANNIVERSARY CAKES

It is not very often that I receive requests for golden wedding anniversary cakes but I sometimes do. Imagine being married for 50 years! This celebration just screams for a special cake. Do a little research and work out which colour or symbol reflects the particular anniversary milestone being celebrated. For example, 50 years is gold, 40 years is ruby, 30 years is pearl and 25 years is silver. Another great idea is to use two sugar figurines to represent the couple. This is a bit more work but it will be much appreciated. Please don't forget that many of the other cake designs in this book might also be suitable, or you may want to make your own cake design using the techniques you have learned. There are no hard-and-fast rules as to what an anniversary cake should be.

DESIGNER RIBBONS

Do you want to make a super-easy two-tier cake? If you want to make it easier still, replace the sugar-paste peony with fresh or fake flowers. You'll be overwhelmed by the choice of gorgeous ribbons you can use. A sweet idea is to use the same colours as the couple had for their wedding theme.

MATERIALS

peony flower (see page 112)

15 cm (6 inch) round cake

20 cm (8 inch) round cake

syrup

1.5 kg (3 lb 5 oz) ganache

15 cm (6 inch) round cake board

20 cm (8 inch) round cake board

25 cm (10 inch) round cake display board (optional)

1.7 kg (3 lb 12 oz) ready-to-roll fondant icing

650 g (1 lb 7 oz) ready-to-roll fondant icing, extra, for display board (optional)

cornflour (cornstarch), for dusting

butchers' skewers, for stacking

2 m (79 inches) of 2.5 cm (1 inch) wide striped ribbon

double-sided adhesive tape

EQUIPMENT

ganaching tools

icing tools

pastry brush

paring knife

turntable

cornflour shaker

pasta machine (optional)

scissors

tape measure

1 Colour the flower paste red and make the petals and leaves for the peony, following the instructions on page 112. Allow to dry for at least 24 hours.

2 Ganache the cake, following the general instructions on how to ganache and prepare round cakes (see page 48). Allow to set overnight.

3 Cover the cake with the fondant icing, following the general instructions on how to cover round cakes (see page 54). Allow to set overnight.

4 If you are using a display board, cover it with the extra fondant icing, following the general instructions on how to cover cake boards (see page 58). Allow to set overnight.

5 Stack the cakes, following the general instructions on how to stack a two-tier cake (see page 60). Carefully transfer the cake to a display stand or covered display board.

TRIM WITH RIBBON

6 Measure the circumference of the cakes using a flexible tape measure to check the lengths of ribbon required.

7 Wrap the ribbon around the base of each tier and adhere with double-sided adhesive tape. Cover the join with a small neat bow.

8 To make a bow cut a 12 cm (4½ inch) length of ribbon and turn it over so the wrong side is facing up. Stick some double-sided adhesive tape in the centre and fold each end over to adhere in the centre. Cut a 4 cm (1½ inch) piece of ribbon to fold over the centre of the bow and secure it at the back with double-sided adhesive tape.

9 Decide on the position of the peony and carefully insert the wire into the cake.

FRANGIPANIS

All couples are different and I make this cake especially for couples who love the beach and all things fresh and lovely. It's young and clean, and you can change the colours to suit your theme. It looks great in bright colours. If you don't wish to have frangipanis, then the top can be left plain or adorned with any of the sugar flowers listed in this book, or if you are feeling really cutesy, two teddy bears look very sweet!

MATERIALS

15 cm (6 inch) round cake
20 cm (8 inch) round cake
syrup
1.4 kg (3 lb 2 oz) ganache
15 cm (6 inch) round cake board
20 cm (8 inch) round cake board
25 cm (10 inch) round cake display board (optional)
2.25 kg (5 lb) ready-to-roll white fondant icing
700 g (1 lb 9 oz) ready-to-roll pale blue fondant icing
650 g (1 lb 7 oz) ready-to-roll fondant icing, extra, for display board (optional)
cornflour (cornstarch), for dusting
butchers' skewers, for stacking
royal icing
7 frangipani flowers, plus extra buds and leaves (see page 116)
50 cm (20 inches) of 10 mm (⅜ inch) wide white satin ribbon

EQUIPMENT

ganaching tools
icing tools
paring knife
paintbrush
pastry brush
pins
turntable
ruler
scissors
pasta machine (optional)
small and large rolling pins
flexiscraper
baking paper
waxed cardboard
2B pencil

1   Ganache the cakes, following the general instructions on how to ganache and prepare round cakes (see page 48). Allow to set overnight.

2   Cover the cakes with the white fondant icing, following the general instructions on how to cover round cakes (see page 54). Allow to set overnight. Reserve the remaining white fondant icing for the lid.

3   If you are using a display board, cover it with the extra fondant icing, following the general instructions on how to cover cake boards (see page 58). Allow to set overnight.

4   Make seven open frangipani flowers and several frangipani buds and leaves from flower paste, following the instructions on page 117. Allow to dry overnight.

5   Make lids for the cakes: the small cake has a lid of pale blue fondant icing and the large cake has a lid of white fondant icing. Follow the general instructions on how to make a lid (see page 86). Reserve the remaining pale blue fondant icing for the stripes.

STRIPES

6   Measure the circumference of the larger cake to work out how wide to make the stripes. To prevent ending with the same colour stripe as you started with, you always need to calculate stripe widths so there is an even number of stripes. On the cake in our picture, we've made the blue stripes slightly wider and the white gaps slightly narrower. Use a tape measure and pin to mark the position of the stripes.

7   Roll out blue fondant icing to approximately 3 mm (⅛ inch) thick and cut stripes to the width you've calculated. You can create a template for the stripes from waxed cardboard, or simply cut them with a pizza cutter and ruler. Place the stripes under a vinyl sheet to keep them from drying out as you work.

8   Carefully brush from the base of the cake to the lip of the lid with a little water. Apply each stripe vertically from the top down, fitting the end flush with the lid and trimming off the excess at the base with a clean knife. Use the straight edge of a ruler to ensure that the stripe is straight. Smooth with a flexiscraper.

FINISHING

9   Stack the cakes, following the general instructions on how to stack a two-tier cake (see page 60). Carefully transfer the cake to a display stand or covered display board.

10 Place the satin ribbon around the base of the smaller cake to cover the join between the two cakes, following the general instructions on page 77.

11 Place the frangipanis on the top of the cake.

ANNIVERSARY ROSE

Lustre dust is a powder that, when applied to fondant icing, gives a glowing finish. Think of it as a blusher for cakes. These dusts come in a variety of finishes, from sparkly to pearlescent. You can apply lustre with a soft dry brush for a shimmer effect—this works well with ivory or white dust; however, in this recipe we use a wet application technique that makes the cake truly glisten and creates depth. Learning how to lustre a cake is an invaluable technique and once you master it you will probably find yourself using it all the time. It will work for many of the cake designs in this book and I encourage you to experiment and have fun with different colours.

MATERIALS

large rose (see page 106)

15 cm (6 inch) round cake

syrup

550 g (1 lb 4 oz) ganache

15 cm (6 inch) round cake board

20 cm (8 inch) round cake display board (optional)

700 g (1 lb 9 oz) ready-to-roll fondant icing

brown food colouring paste (optional)

500 g (1 lb 2 oz) ready-to-roll fondant icing, extra, for display board (optional)

2–3 tablespoons copper lustre dust

60–125 ml (2–2 ½ fl oz / ¼–½ cup) cake decorator's alcohol

70 cm (27½ inches) of 10 mm (⅜ inch) wide copper satin ribbon, for display board or stand

glue stick or double-sided adhesive tape

50 cm (20 inches) of 10 mm (⅜ inch) wide copper satin ribbon, extra, for cake (optional)

cornflour (cornstarch), for dusting

EQUIPMENT

ganaching tools

icing tools

small bowl

palette knife

2 pastry brushes

large soft paintbrush

turntable (optional)

1   Make the petals and leaves for the rose, following the instructions on page 106. Allow to dry for at least 24 hours before assembling.

2   Ganache the cake, following the general instructions on how to ganache and prepare round cakes (see page 48). Allow to set overnight.

3   Colour the ready-to-roll fondant icing, following the instructions on page 72, or simply use it without colouring. Cover the cake with the fondant icing, following the general instructions on how to cover round cakes (see page 54). Allow to set overnight.

4   If using a covered display board, use the extra fondant icing to cover the board following the general instructions on how to cover display boards (see page 58). Allow to set overnight.

The lustre effect will be deeper and richer if you colour the fondant icing to match the shade of the lustre dust. For this copper finish, you could use brown icing.

WET LUSTRE

5   Mix 1 tablespoon of lustre dust with 60 ml (2 fl oz/¼ cup) of decorator's alcohol, using a small bowl and a palette knife. You will need to work very quickly before the lustre dries out.

6   Start with the top of the cake, using a pastry brush to quickly apply the wet lustre and making sure the brush strokes are going in one direction. Before the lustre dries, dry brush it with a dry pastry brush or soft paintbrush to clean up the brush strokes. If required you can apply a second coat immediately, before the lustre dries, by repeating the process.

7   After you have completed the top of the cake, apply lustre to the side as a wet coat and then brush with a dry brush. Work in horizontal strokes around the cake rather than up and down: this is where a turntable will be invaluable. Repeat with a second coat immediately, if required.

If the mixture thickens, use more cake decorator's alcohol to soften it. For tiered cakes, lustre one tier at a time before stacking; for square cakes, complete one side at a time.

8   Make sure the cake is completely dry before moving it onto the display stand or display board. Use a glue stick or double-sided adhesive tape to adhere ribbon around the edge of the display stand. You can also apply ribbon around the base of the cake if you wish, following the general instructions on page 77.

9   Assemble the sugar rose, allow to dry and place it carefully on top of the cake.

LOVE BIRDS CAKE

This is one of my favourite cakes—the combination of the birds and the ruffles is cute. Learning how to make flower ruffles will be such an important skill as a decorator; you can use them with many designs in this book and they look particularly good on the bottom layer of a tiered cake. The figurines are very simple; however, you could replace them with flowers or coloured ribbons.

MATERIALS

18 cm (7 inch) round cake

syrup

650 g (1 lb 7 oz) ganache

18 cm (7 inch) round cake board

23 cm (9 inch) round cake display board (optional)

1 kg (2 lb 4 oz) ready-to-roll fondant icing

600 g (1 lb 5 oz) ready-to-roll fondant icing, extra, for display board (optional)

500 g (1 lb 2 oz) ready-to-roll fondant icing, extra, for flower ruffles

love bird figurines (see page 99)

cornflour (cornstarch), for dussting

70 cm (27½ inches) of satin ribbon (optional)

sugar glue

EQUIPMENT

ganaching tools

icing tools

paring knife

barbecue skewers

toothpicks

small and large rolling pins

leaf cutters

small and medium paintbrushes

circle cutter set

modelling tools

1 Ganache the cake, following the general instructions on how to ganache and prepare round cakes (see page 48). Allow to set overnight.

2 Cover the cake with the fondant icing, following the general instructions on how to cover round cakes (see page 54). Allow to set overnight.

3 Cover the display board, if using, with the fondant icing, following the general instructions on how to cover display boards (see page 58). Allow to set overnight. Trim the board with ribbon.

4 Carefully transfer the cake to a display stand or covered display board.

FLOWER RUFFLES

5 Roll out the fondant icing for the flower ruffles to about 2 mm (1⁄16 inch) thick. If the icing is too thin the flowers will 'wilt'. Use a circle cutter to cut out small circles and keep them under a vinyl sheet so they don't dry out.

6 Create 'flowers' by pinching a circle at one edge to create a petal shape. Put 5 petals together and use your fingers to squeeze them together at the base. Make a few flowers at a time.

7 Use a medium paintbrush to place a dab of water and adhere each flower to the cake. Arrange the flowers close together, making sure there are no gaps in your arrangement. Work on a small section at a time.

8 Use toothpicks to support the weight of the petals until the flowers are dry enough to support themselves.

9 Repeat around the entire cake.

FIGURINES

11 Make the love birds, following the instructions on page 99. They need to be placed on the cake while they are still soft so that the skewers or toothpicks for support can pass through the log.

APPENDIX:
GANACHE AND ICING QUANTITIES

CAKE SIZE	GANACHE (ROUND)	GANACHE (SQUARE)
13 cm (5 inch)	395 g (13¾ oz)	500 g (1 lb 2 oz)
15 cm (6 inch)	515 g (1 lb 2½ oz)	655 g (1 lb 7 oz)
18 cm (7 inch)	650 g (1 lb 7 oz)	830 g (1 lb 13½ oz)
20 cm (8 inch)	800 g (1 lb 12 oz)	1020 g (2 lb 5 oz)
23 cm (9 inch)	965 g (2 lb 2½ oz)	1230 g (2 lb 12 oz)
25 cm (10 inch)	1145 g (2 lb 8½ oz)	1455 g (3 lb 4 oz)
27.5 cm (11 inch)	1340 g (3 lb 1 oz)	1700 g (3 lb 12 oz)
30 cm (12 inch)	1545 g (3 lb 6½ oz)	1965 g (4 lb 5 oz)

CAKE SIZE	READY-TO-ROLL FONDANT ICING (ROUND)	READY-TO-ROLL FONDANT ICING (SQUARE)
15 cm (6 inch)	700 g (1 lb 9 oz)	850 g (1 lb 14 oz)
20 cm (8 inch)	1 kg (2 lb 4 oz)	1.25 kg (2 lb 12 oz)
25 cm (10 inch)	1.5 kg (3 lb 5 oz)	1.75 kg (3 lb 14 oz)
30 cm (12 inch)	1.6 kg (3 lb 8 oz)	2.1 kg (4 lb 4 oz)

DISPLAY BOARD SIZE	READY-TO-ROLL FONDANT ICING (ROUND)	READY-TO-ROLL FONDANT ICING (SQUARE)
15 cm (6 inch)	200 g (7 oz)	250 g (9 oz)
18 cm (7 inch)	300 g (10½ oz)	400 g (14 oz)
20 cm (8 inch)	500 g (1 lb 2 oz)	550 g (1 lb 4 oz)
23 cm (9 inch)	600 g (1 lb 5 oz)	650 g (1 lb 7 oz)
25 cm (10 inch)	650 g (1 lb 7 oz)	700 g (1 lb 9 oz)
27.5 cm (11 inch)	700 g (1 lb 9 oz)	725 g 1 lb 9½ oz)
30 cm (12 inch)	750 g(1 lb 10 oz)	850 g (1 lb 14 oz)
35 cm (14 inch)	900 g (2 lb)	1 kg (2 lb 4 oz)

ACKNOWLEDGEMENTS

Technical books like this one usually take a long time to put together and this book took the better part of two years to write. Therefore there are many people whom I need to thank, some who were with me for part of the process and some who held my hand the whole way through. They all deserve a very special mention.

Firstly, thank you to my publisher, Diana Hill, for always believing in this book and in me; for being endlessly patient and a delight to work with. I have often thought how lucky I have been to work with you: I am not sure I would have been nearly as kind and supportive as you have been.

A big thank you to my editor, Melody Lord. You must have the patience of Job working with someone as harebrained as me; however, this manuscript would not be what it is without your patience and skill.

Thank you also to my managing editors: to Barbara McClenahan for overseeing such a huge process and bringing this book to life, and to Katie Bosher for seeing the book safely through the final stages.

I must express my gratitude to an amazing design team. To my photographer Chris Chen, I loved working with you and your beautiful images made this book; thank you so much. To Vanessa Austin, my stylist, what can I say? You make everything so lovely! Vivien Valk: I have worked with you on five books now and I trust you completely, you are a star and legend in the publishing world and you deserve to be. And big thank you to Arielle Gamble for doing such a beautiful job of designing this book.

I would like to say thank you to a very talented team of decorators who helped me get through the biggest photo shoot I have ever had. Jo Pike, Kirstie Blain, Jin-Hee Park, Carole Ford and Debbi-Lee Russell. You are all amazing, kind and gifted in your own right: I am sure you will all go on to do great things in the cake world. You were incredibly supportive of me and I appreciate it greatly.

For their design contributions, a big thank you to my head designer and dear friend Antony Bullimore for our Vintage Ruffles Cake, PC intern Lori Filannino for the Jewelled Flowers and PC Production Manager Debbi-Lee Russell for her You're so Sweet design. They were just too good not to include, thank you!

Thank you to Luke Olsen, owner of Cake Decorating Solutions (www.cakedecoratingsolutions.com.au) for supplying all of the materials and equipment required to create this book.

Thank you to Sweet Splash Backdrops for the use of your backdrops, found on Etsy. Additional props were supplied by Paper Couture; Dulux; Wedgwood; Spotlight; Bespoke Balloonery; Emerald and Ella; and South Pacific Fabrics.

Finally and most importantly I want to thank my husband, Ahmad. I cannot even imagine how much patience you must have to sit through endless hours of my writing, procrastinating and surviving a four-week-long photo shoot. You are my rock and my greatest supporter, and will always be my greatest love.

INDEX

Page numbers in *italics* refer to photographs.

Published in 2015 by Murdoch Books, an imprint of Allen & Unwin

Murdoch Books Australia
83 Alexander Street
Crows Nest NSW 2065
Phone: +61 (0)2 8425 0100
Fax: +61 (0)2 9906 2218
murdochbooks.com.au
info@murdochbooks.com.au

Murdoch Books UK
Erico House, 6th Floor
93–99 Upper Richmond Road
Putney, London SW15 2TG
Phone: +44 (0) 20 8785 5995
murdochbooks.co.uk
info@murdochbooks.co.uk

For Corporate Orders & Custom Publishing contact
Noel Hammond, National Business Development Manager, Murdoch Books Australia

Publisher: Diana Hill
Editorial Managers: Barbara McClenahan and Katie Bosher
Design Manager: Vivien Valk
Project Editor: Melody Lord
Designer: Arielle Gamble
Photographer: Chris Chen
Stylist: Vanessa Austin
Food Editor: Grace Campbell
Production Manager: Mary Bjelobrk

Text © Paris Cutler 2015
The moral rights of the author have been asserted.
Design © Murdoch Books 2015
Photography © Chris Chen 2015 [except photography on pages: 12, 38, 41, 46-50, 52, 55-57, 68-71, 73-75, 78, 79, 82, 88 and 89 by Natasha Milne © Murdoch Books 2009]

A cataloguing-in-publication entry is available from the catalogue of the National Library of Australia at nla.gov.au.

ISBN 978 1 74336 094 1 Australia
ISBN 978 1 74336 058 3 UK

A catalogue record for this book is available from the British Library.

Colour reproduction by Splitting Image Colour Studio Pty Ltd, Clayton, Victoria
Printed by 1010 Printing International Limited, China

IMPORTANT: *Those who might be at risk from the effects of salmonella poisoning (the elderly, pregnant women, young children and those suffering from immune deficiency diseases) should consult their doctor with any concerns about eating raw eggs.*

OVEN GUIDE: *You may find cooking times vary depending on the oven you are using. For fan-forced ovens, as a general rule, set the oven temperature to 20°C (35°F) lower than indicated in the recipe.*

MEASURES GUIDE: *We have used 20 ml (4 teaspoon) tablespoon measures. If you are using a 15 ml (3 teaspoon) tablespoon add an extra teaspoon of the ingredient for each tablespoon specified.*